Praise for
Playdates with God

"Something profoundly happens... psychologist's mind and a poet's heart. You'll find that glorious intersection here, in *Playdates with God*. This book is a thoughtful and lyrical exploration of what it means to fall in love with God all over again—and to stay in love. Read this book, and recover your joy."

—**Jennifer Dukes Lee,** author of *Love Idol*

"*Playdates with God* is more than a book. It is a prayer, reaching deep into the soul and evoking intimacy, joy, and childlike faith. Laura Boggess tenderly carves out a space for those who've been hurt, by church and life, to rediscover the love of God through poetry, transparency, and insight. This is a must-read for those with restless hearts, longing to find their way home."

—**Emily T. Wierenga,** author of *Chasing Silhouettes* and *Atlas Girl*
(www.emilywierenga.com)

"*Playdates with God* beckons us to something new, yet still familiar. It is a reminder that life and spirituality are not just the chores, spreadsheets, and appointment books that make up much of adult life. Connecting with God is about playing, laughing, and exploring the way we did as children. In fact, making time for play, for silliness, for laughter is so paradoxically important, such serious business that we simply must stop neglecting it as a true spiritual practice."

—**Matt Appling,** educator, pastor, author of *Life After Art: What Your Forgot About Life and Faith Since You Left the Art Room*

"With Laura Boggess's sudden epiphany that 'Our world is not wired for wonder,' a quest is born—a quest to awaken her hunger for wonder, for the God-joy she once knew as a child but has long forgotten as an adult. Journey with Laura as *Playdates with God* unfolds, awakening to wonder as she sees and experiences it and delighting in the breathtaking beauty of the extraordinary ordinary. Laura Boggess glimpses beauty in the everyday and then weaves these riches into ethereal vignettes, transporting the reader to a place where heaven meets earth and God shimmers within reach. *Playdates with God* is a book you'll want to read slowly, savoring each rich image, lingering over each lyrical word, and satisfying your hunger for the wonder you have missed."

—**Michelle DeRusha,** author of *Spiritual Misfit: A Memoir of Uneasy Faith*

"'Number three seemed invisible. Nothing special,' Boggess says of her birth order. Perhaps this very impression of invisibility is what gave the author space to develop an unusual depth of observation. If Boggess began as nothing special, then her peerings into the world and the soul have righted that once and for all. Her gift of words is special indeed."

—**Laura L. Barkat,** CEO and managing editor of Tweetspeak Poetry and author of *Rumors of Water: Thoughts on Creativity & Writing*

"Laura Boggess invites us into intimacy with God in the everyday moments of life. This intimacy is not about striving but rather enjoying, not about laboring but instead being loved, not about losing ourselves but about finally being found in the ways we've longed for all our lives. Let Laura's beautiful words and gentle wisdom guide your heart closer to the One who has been with you all along."

—**Holley Gerth,** best-selling author of *You're Already Amazing*

"Laura Boggess is an incredibly gifted writer, in command of a uniquely lyrical and poetic voice. She paints pictures with words and lures us out of our hiding places, reminding us that God invites our spontaneous, simple, honest, and earnest praise. Even (especially?) when our praise takes the shape of squirt guns, or trampolines, or heartfelt prayers with our forehead pressed to the dining room floor. Laura is a gentle teacher, and we are better because she took the time to show us the way."

—**Deidra Riggs,** managing editor at *The High Calling*

"*Playdates with God* is an invitation to pray . . . and to play. With a lyrical, poetic style, Laura Boggess expresses her deep longing for more of God—a longing which sets her playdates in motion. I daresay this book will awaken the same longing in each of us, setting our own playdates in motion. After reading *Playdates with God,* we'll find ourselves wide-eyed with wonder, jumping with abandon on a neighbor's trampoline—breathless with joy and closer than ever to the God of the universe."

—**Ann Kroeker,** author of *Not So Fast: Slow-Down Solutions for Frenzied Families*

"'How do I come to Jesus like a child?' This is the question Laura Boggess explores—playfully, seriously, earnestly, poetically, beautifully, and insightfully—in *Playdates with God.* Drawing upon a depth of personal experience and a breadth of writers, Boggess offers illuminating answers that beckon us toward a childlike sense of wonder and delight that suits every stage of life. After reading *Playdates with God,* you'll never view suitcases, see-saws, or Super Soakers the same way again!"

—**Karen Swallow Prior,** author of *Booked: Literature in the Soul of Me* and *Fierce Convictions: The Extraordinary Life of Hannah More—Poet, Reformer, Abolitionist*

"Many of us have forgotten the life-giving joys of play. When we lose our child-*like*-ness, we become child-*ish* — and that causes so much misbehavior and misery. Thank God for Laura Boggess's testimony. Boggess shows us that, through humility and the hard work of remembering, we can correct our distorted posture and return to a state of wonder. She's asking you to come out and play. Do yourself a favor and accept the invitation."

—**Jeffrey Overstreet,** author of *Auralia's Colors* and *Through a Screen Darkly* (www.lookingcloser.org)

Playdates
with GOD

Playdates with GOD

Having a Childlike Faith in a Grown-up World

Laura Boggess

LEAFWOOD
PUBLISHERS
an imprint of Abilene Christian University Press

PLAYDATES WITH GOD
Having a Childlike Faith in a Grown-up World

LEAFWOOD
P U B L I S H E R S
an imprint of Abilene Christian University Press

Copyright © 2014 by Laura Boggess

ISBN 978-0-89112-620-1 | LCCN 2014024906

Printed in the United States of America

Published in association with William K. Jensen Literary Agency, 119 Bampton Court, Eugene, Oregon 97404.

LIBRARY OF CONGRESS CATALOGING-IN-PUBLICATION DATA
Boggess, Laura, 1969-
  Playdates with God : having a childlike faith in a grownup world / Laura Boggess.
     pages cm
  Includes bibliographical references and index.
  ISBN 978-0-89112-620-1 (alk. paper)
  1. God (Christianity)--Worship and love. 2. Spirituality--Christianity. 3. Spiritual life--Christianity. I. Title.
  BV4817.B575 2014
  231.7--dc23

                                                                                        2014024906

Cover design by Jenette Munger | Interior text design by Sandy Armstrong, Strong Design

For information contact:
Leafwood Publishers, an imprint of Abilene Christian University Press
1626 Campus Court, Abilene, Texas 79601

1-877-816-4455 | www.leafwoodpublishers.com

14 15 16 17 18 19 / 7 6 5 4 3 2 1

In memory of Lucy Mae—my little petal—
the most faithful friend and sweetest of critics.

contents

in humble gratitude

The gifts bestowed by others in the making of this book cast a long shadow, and I am so grateful for all those who stand in the light and have held my hand in the dark through this journey.

Bill Jensen, these words would never have spilled onto the page if not for your conviction that they should be shared. Thank you for your friendship. Thank you, also, to the good people at Leafwood Publishers. What a privilege it has been to work with you.

To Laura Barkat, who first believed in my voice and whose own rich voice schooled me in the many ways of the writing life. I am so glad God brought us together. To Maureen Doallas, who first put forth the idea of *Playdates with God* as a book and whose poetry has been my muse on many a day. I'm ever grateful to my blogging community, to every reader and writer who has shared his or her own playdates with God on my blog. What a gift to hold your stories in my heart.

To the community at The High Calling—you know who you are—who could have known what beauty God would knit together when the idea of "online community" was first conceived? I have found real, deep friendships with some of you I have never "met" and some I have been privileged to behold in person after a lengthy online relationship. Only God. Only God could do such a thing. You are beautiful. A special thank you to my fellow High Calling editors—from you I learn and am inspired every day. And especially to Marcus Goodyear and Deidra Riggs, whom I adore and whose friendships I treasure.

To my writer's group mates Melissa Beckford and Verbieanne Helyger—I love you girls. Thank you for reading, for believing in me, and for loving me.

My small group and Bible study friends at Teays Valley Presbyterian Church—your prayers have sustained me. Thank you for the ways you've helped me grow and learn and kept me accountable. What a privilege to do life with you all.

To my family—Mom, Dad, and all my siblings—your love has been the soil bed for much of the beauty in my life. Thank you for sticking with me, for all the grace you've given.

Ted and Ada Boggess, how blessed I was when I married your son to gain two such wonderful parents. Thank you for all the ways you have supported me over the years but, mostly, thank you for loving my children so well.

Teddy and Jeffrey—where you are, there my heart is also. Oh, how I love you. What a gift God has given me in you, in this mother-love.

Jeff. My love. How to name the ways your love has given to me? I'm so grateful to be weaving this story with you. You are God's gift to me.

Above all, to my Lord and Savior, my heart is yours. You are the Blue Flower—my *Blaue Blume*—the Beauty that fills.

preface

the blue flower

I am Eve. I hold the world in my womb. My belly swells with generations who will call me mother, and my hands carve out a place that those I love will always call home. My heart shelters and nourishes all that is beautiful and holy in my small world. I give much and I receive much. I am loved.

I have walked in the cool of the shade with the Almighty and yet . . . this is not enough. I hunger for more. This hunger . . . how it consumes. Sometimes I wonder: Is this the hunger of Eve? When I think of Paradise, I wonder that one who was given so much could want for more. Whatever could she have longed for that was not already hers? And yet . . . am I not the same? I take the gift of my life with one hand and hold the other out to receive more. Always, always wanting.

My own humble beginnings make me wonder if Eve struggled with not being first. Did she feel—somehow—that she was not enough? That being second made her second best? Did the lie the serpent fed her speak to a deep hunger—the fear that she would not be loved—not completely? If only she had this one thing, would she somehow feel whole? And if wisdom was her apple, what is mine?

If this aching emptiness is so ingrained in my DNA that its thread can be followed back to the first man and woman . . . what hope do I have of filling that cavernous well? I am a daughter of Eve and I reach with tremulous hands for forbidden fruit. I have believed the lie that this hunger that is so much a part of me means I am not enough.

I was born the third child of four to a working-class family and tired parents. My birth order allotted no privileges. The first-born—my brother—would be doted on and favored his whole life. The second—my sister—had the particularity of being the first girl. And my little brother? Well, he was the baby. Number three seemed . . . invisible. Nothing special, for sure. At least it felt that way to a blue-eyed, freckle-faced girl who would spend most of her young life trying to be seen—searching for more than just being the invisible number three.

When I was a young woman, this longing to be seen sent me wandering down a shadowy path, arms flung out before me in the darkness—feeling my way inch by precarious inch. Seeking to sate the quivering hunger.

The paths I chose were the paths of fleeting fulfillment. I was left emptier than before—scarred and filled with regrets. Reeling, I learned to ignore the yearning—patch over the hole with things and people and busyness. It wasn't to be trusted, this deep soul-desire. I learned to pretend that I wasn't carrying around a pit inside of me. I began to think there was something wrong with me. Would I never be happy? What was with these sudden storms that passed through me and over me, leaving such devastation in their wake?

It was in the aftermath of this self-destructive season that I switched directions. I would become a rule-follower, and this would be my salvation. I went from one extreme to the next, as legalists often do. But neither did my soul find rest there. After the list failed me—when the rule-following only seemed to stoke the hunger—I turned to books. They were my refuge as a child, and what question could not be answered in a book? And what better book than the Bible—the book I turn to for all comfort? I read it straight through, recording great chunks of it in my journal and memorizing bits and pieces.

What I found, though, was not necessarily an answer to this hunger inside—no checklist there—but more an understanding. Stories of seeking, failing, and falling into grace-filled love.

I read the story of David over and over—all his triumphs and heartbreaking failures. He became my hero. He made such grievous mistakes—adultery, murder, poor parenting—and still did not shrink from the love of God. Could I allow myself—the invisible number three—to be loved like that? The naming of the emptiness seemed on the tip of my tongue, and the evidence was right there in the Psalms.

"O Lord, all my longing is known to you; my sighing is not hidden from you. My heart throbs, my strength fails me; as for the light of my eyes—it also has gone from me" (Ps. 38:9–10 NRSV).

"My soul languishes for your salvation; I hope in your word. My eyes fail with watching for your promise; I ask, 'When will you comfort me?'" (Ps. 119:81–82 NRSV).

And Paul spoke these words while he was in Athens, teaching the city's leading philosophers about God:

> The God who made the world and everything in it, he who is Lord of heaven and earth, does not live in shrines made by human hands, nor is he served by human hands, as though he needed anything, since he himself gives to all mortals life and breath and all things. From one ancestor he made all nations to inhabit the whole earth, and he allotted the times of their existence and the boundaries of the places where they would live, so that they would search for God and perhaps grope for him and find him—though indeed he is not far from each one of us. (Acts 17:24–27 NRSV)

Was this what I had been feeling all my life? Groping for God?

On the pages of history, I found kindred spirits—ancient words named me, and my heart found a home inside the prayers of saints long passed. Why this surprised me, I do not know. Isn't Eve the mother of us all? Aren't we all made from the same dust? I discovered hearts that beat in tandem with mine.

I picked up Saint Augustine's *Confessions*—the book the venerable African bishop penned between AD 397 and AD 398, thought to be the first Western autobiography written—and there, on the first page, the very beginning lines: "You stir man to take pleasure in praising you, because you have made us for yourself, and our heart is restless until it rests in you" (3).

When I first read these words, I put my hand to my heart, felt its steady beating, and was swept away to meet this man who lived centuries before me—a mother, wife, worker person . . . a regular gal—and I knew: he felt the very same longings as I.

Have you felt them, too? It's the sigh in your spirit when the sun makes shine on water, the twist in your heart when you walk under a star-filled sky; it's the music—so beautiful—that haunts you in your sleep, the curve of a baby's cheek, that feeling of small under a forest canopy, the scent of earth filling your nostrils; it's the way the ocean sings as it strums over a shell-strewn shore . . . the awakening to beauty everywhere. Have you felt these longings? And what have you done with them? Wrestled them into submission? Swept them under the rug? Drowned them in alcohol? I tried all of these and more—turning to people and things, experiences, knowledge, emulating the lives of others . . . and still these longings pulsed inside of me, taking on a life of their own and urging me forward in that quest to fill.

But Augustine and these other saints I was meeting for the first time? They felt these very same longings. They recognized them for what they are. *And they wrote about them.* They filled books with their heart thoughts so that people like me—and you—might not think we're insane.

In his renowned defense of the Christian religion, *Pensées,* the seventeenth-century French philosopher and mathematician Blaise Pascal says:

> What is it, then, that this desire and this inability
> proclaim to us, but that there was once in man a true
> happiness of which there now remain to him only the

mark and empty trace, which he in vain tries to fill
from all his surroundings, seeking from things absent
the help he does not obtain in things present? But
these are all inadequate, because the infinite abyss
can only be filled by an infinite and immutable object,
that is to say, only by God Himself. (Kindle edition,
2205–10)

The God-shaped hole.

But it was not until I discovered the works of Clive Staples
Lewis that my heart found its glad companion. Mr. Lewis wrote
freely and frequently about his own yearning—and he gave me a
word to name it: *sehnsucht.* This German word does not translate
well to English, but it can best be defined as nostalgia, or a deep
longing for a far-off home. From one of his letters:

About death I go through different moods, but the
times when I can desire it are never, I think, those
when this world seems harshest. On the contrary, it is
just when there seems to be most of Heaven already
here that I come nearest to longing for a *patria.* It is
the bright frontispiece which whets one to read the
story itself. All joy (as distinct from mere pleasure,
still more amusement) emphasizes our pilgrim status;
always reminds, beckons, awakens desire. Our best
havings are wantings. (*Letters of C. S. Lewis,* 289)

Our best havings are wantings. Lewis's words beckoned me to
embrace this sehnsucht. He likened it to a call to our heavenly
home—an otherworldly sense of joy.

Lewis's views of sehnsucht were influenced by the work of the German poet and philosopher Novalis and the American author and clergyman Henry van Dyke. Novalis's unfinished romance *Heinrich von Ofterdingen* introduces us to the hero of that name. The story opens with Heinrich musing over an earlier meeting with a stranger who is also a storyteller. The stranger shows Heinrich a blue flower that the young man cannot stop thinking about. Later, Heinrich dreams a wonderful dream about the blue flower that awakens a lifelong yearning to find the elusive bloom. As the readers, we recognize that the yearning is about more than the blue flower; the blue flower is unattainable—the search is futile. Novalis's story of unfulfilled longing so moved a generation that the blue flower became the symbol of German Romanticism. Novalis died of tuberculosis at age twenty-eight in 1801, before completing the work.

But his story of the blue flower inspired another writer one hundred years later. In the preface of his collection of short stories, *The Blue Flower,* Henry van Dyke says of the title, "I have borrowed a symbol from the old German poet and philosopher, Novalis, to stand instead of a name. The Blue Flower which he used in his romance of Heinrich von Ofterdingen to symbolise Poetry, the object of his young hero's quest, I have used here to signify happiness, the satisfaction of the heart" (Preface).

In the works of both Novalis and van Dyke, the blue flower is not the point . . . it is merely the representation of this yearning, this seeking . . . this sehnsucht. The appeal of the story is the desire—not the object of it. As Lewis said, *our best havings are wantings.*

These three, all men of deep faith, understood that this longing was designed for a higher purpose. "All joy . . . emphasizes our pilgrim status; always reminds, beckons, awakens desire," says Lewis.

This desire that hums inside of me—it has a purpose. It reminds me that I am on a journey, that I was created for more.

I think about the beginning of hunger—the first groping for more—and I wonder . . . what if Eve had recognized this desire for what it is? What if she let the hunger be the compass to point her back to the One who can fill every longing?

And how do I do this? What if . . . what if I could learn from our mother Eve? What if I recognized that this hunger—this desire—is good? That it is the very thing that drives me deeper in intimacy to my good God.

So history is rich with stories of those who wrestled with this restlessness long before me. But these three men were my early companions as I, too, began my search for the blue flower. For Novalis, it was poetry. For van Dyke? Happiness. And Lewis searched long for joy. But me? I see the sehnsucht in something that frequently encompasses all of these. To me, the sehnsucht is that crazy, wild, giddy feeling of falling in love.

Over and over and over again.

trampoline

It all started with the trampoline.

The day was white with February dawning, and I stepped out into it—thick wet flakes falling one by one from a thin gray heaven and pooling on my skin, wetting my hair and making me blink. It was the in-between time, with the holidays well behind us and spring still six weeks away.

Walking in the snow has always been cause for celebration, but this day? Winter was tired. Icy fingers stroked my bones, and when the season's melancholy seemed to reach its deepest ebb . . . I heard them. Children's voices calling through the snow. Their laughter echoed—sliding between those big wet flakes through the neighborhood streets until it found a home in my waiting ear. I followed the echo through the yard, across the street, and to its source at the house behind. I peeked. Two boys—soaked to the skin, jumping on a trampoline. As I watched those boys frolic and giggle and slide onto their backs on that trampoline in the snow, something moved inside of me.

I am not a fan of the trampoline. I work at a medical rehabilitation hospital—with those who have suffered spinal cord injuries and brain injuries. I know the statistics. The trampoline is a culprit. But I watched in wonder as those boys popcorned each other up and down, and all rational thought took flight . . . I remembered.

I remembered how it feels not to be anchored by everything learned over these long years. I remembered how it feels to be a child—to live in innocence, a stranger to fear. I watched those boys bound up and down, laughter bubbling over with each flight, and felt a nudge in my spirit. And something else.

I yearned.

I yearned for that kind of unself-consciousness. I wondered about it. Was this the way it was in the Garden? When Adam and Eve walked unashamed in their nakedness, was their day-to-day covered in this freedom also? That unrestrained joy was familiar and foreign all at once. Could it be that I was made for this? This recognition—is this what psychiatrist Carl Jung meant by the collective unconscious? That place that God carves in us . . . a knowledge . . . a collection of numinous memories we all share?

Is this the way our moments are meant to be spent? This wild joy—unashamed?

All week long, I thought about the trampoline.

What is it about catching that free air—that sky jump that lifts endlessly? Is it the way we leave the earth behind? Does it shake loose the bindings of this loamy existence? I couldn't seem to help myself; I kept thinking about the trampoline. The memory would break in at the oddest times—when interviewing a patient at the hospital where I work, at church on Sunday morning in the middle of my pastor's sermon, when I kissed my husband good-bye each morning and closed the door behind me . . . even in my dreams at night. I would fly—soar weightlessly in reckless joy.

They felt like an invitation, those bouncy thoughts. God was inviting me to play, and it made me nervously giddy. Nevertheless, on my next day off, after I took my two boys to school, I retraced the steps that had followed that breadcrumb trail of laughter. I had a good talk with God on the way, too. *My neighbor is sweet, Lord,* I said, *but she may just think I've lost my mind.*

Then I thought of something that nearly made me turn around.

What if her husband answers the door?

I rehearsed my lines.

May I play on your trampoline?

Too weird.

I'm doing this thing, playing with God and, well, he told me to jump on your trampoline.

Take me to the funny farm now.

With no plan, I approached the door. In fear and trembling, I delicately put finger to doorbell.

No answer.

I peered through the dark windows.

What now, Lord?

Cautiously, I walked around the house to the backyard. I couldn't believe what my treacherous mind was contemplating.

Is it against the law to jump on someone else's trampoline without permission? I knew my neighbor wouldn't mind, but still . . .

I slipped off my shoes. Clambered up in the awkward way of a fortyish woman.

And I did. I jumped. Slow at first, but with each landing on the heel—each pushing off with the balls of the feet—I went higher. This body shed free the years, and I became unfettered. I became a stranger in my body, but I remembered. Oh, yes, I remembered this. There was sun-warmed elastic beneath my bare feet, and I was loosed to bound free. The earth fell below, and I flew.

The laughter came when I remembered the boys, and I fell in a heap of giggles. There was no snow, only sun and sky, and I could see heaven from where I lay—still and cradled in that elastic womb. And when the laughter hushed and there was just me and God, all tangled up under that blue sky, I made a promise. I promised God that I would not forget the sweetness of that moment. I made a commitment to seek out moments like this with him. Once a week I would leave my grown-up notions behind, and I would find a place where joy and wonder would lead. A playdate with God. I didn't know what that would look like, but I knew it would mean doing faith a little differently. I did not know how hard I would have fight to keep hold of this promise. I did not know how the people I love would smile and pat my hand condescendingly when I dared to mention running after God in this way. Our world is not wired for wonder.

Not for grown-ups, anyway.

But still, it happened months ago, and I can't forget it. The promise I made on the trampoline has been changing me. I can't explain it except to say that the unfettering awakened in me a hunger for the forgotten God-joy. A need to come to him open and trusting, like a little child. In the confines of my grown-up life, I have left behind this feeling—this wonder and freedom that comes with slipping off my shoes and . . . jumping.

ii

born

let's play outside (of the box)

The days are growing longer. I feel them stretch out beneath me and winter sleeps. It is the first day of spring, the vernal equinox—one of two days a year when the sun shines directly on the equator, and the length of day and night are nearly equal in all parts of the world. My crocuses have poked sleepy faces through their covers; the earth awakens in her bed. I feel the deep quiver, the thaw dripping into the belly of the inner core. When I drive to work in the mornings, light follows me slowly. The day dawns like a loom—a series of threads woven through the clouds; the sun peeks and her rays crisscross in daedal strands. I drive into this gauzy gossamer, and the road beneath is chatoyant silk. I am lost in folds and seams and undulating panels.

Standing on this vernal equinox is a strange sort of out-of-balance balance. Day and night may have worked out their differences, but the coming of spring always awakens in me this unsettled desire. In fact, it happens with each change of season—as the earth dons her new cloak, I find myself with this stirring . . . this craving for the new.

It is a feeling with which I am well familiar—this longing. This ever-presence is an ache inside that has grown with me through the years. Sometimes I wonder if this is what is left of my memory of being born—this pull between the staying and leaving. There is the warm comfort of the womb . . . cradled security. But then come the soft contractions, a deep pull—a knowing that there is something more. This tugging grows stronger, squeezing on me until I feel I cannot breathe. And I am thrust into a new world.

Born.

Is there always such pain and discomfort when leaving one world behind and entering another?

When Jesus met with Nicodemus in secret, he told the Pharisee something of this.

"I tell you the truth," he said. "No one can see the kingdom of God unless he is born again."

And Nicodemus, in the cover of darkness—from out of that cloak of legalism—asks, "How can a man be born when he is old? Surely he cannot enter a second time into his mother's womb to be born!" (John 3:3–4 NIV 1984).

Don't I ask this same question? Isn't it when I am smothered by the darkness of the tedium of life that I resist the pull to leave the womb of safety and find resurrected life?

How can this woman be born when she is old?

The scribes and Pharisees of Jesus' day were regarded as the utmost example of righteousness. They were the experts on the law. When we think of "the law," we think of the Ten Commandments that God gave to Moses on those infamous stone tablets. If we're really with it, we might refer to all the mandates of the Old Testament when we discuss the law. Even the more obscure ones like which four-footed winged insects are forbidden to eat (Lev. 11:20–23) or not wearing clothing woven with two kinds of material (Lev. 19:19). But to the scribes and Pharisees of Jesus' day, the law encompassed so much more. It was their job to interpret and keep track of all the traditions and judgments pertaining to the laws that were handed down from one generation to the next.

To be entrusted with such a task requires a serious response, and these experts took their job to heart—often focusing on the tiniest of details to give definition to the law. William Barclay, in his Bible commentary *The Gospel of Matthew*, gives us an idea of just how tedious the process must have been.

> The law lays it down that the Sabbath Day is to be kept
> holy, and that on it no work is to be done. That is a
> great principle. But the Jewish legalists had a passion
> for definition. So they asked: "What is work?"
> All kinds of things were classified as work. For
> instance, *to carry a burden* on the Sabbath Day is
> to work. But next a burden has to be defined. So the
> scribal law lays it down that a burden is "food equal
> in weight to a dried fig, enough wine for mixing in a
> goblet, milk enough for one swallow, honey enough

to put upon a wound, oil enough to anoint a small
member, water enough to moisten an eye-salve,
paper enough to write a custom-house notice upon,
ink enough to write two letters of the alphabet, reed
enough to make a pen"—and so on endlessly. (148)

These traditions—passed down orally from one generation to the next—were written down for the first time in the third century AD, a compilation known as the *Mishnah*. Barclay notes that, translated to English, the Mishnah makes a book of about eight hundred pages.

These are the rules that Nicodemus labored under. Eight hundred pages of mind-numbing, nitpicking minutiae. Even today, in this modern world, there are those days burdened with the "ought tos" and the "musts" and the "have tos." On those days, I think I understand a small bit of why the hearts of so many Pharisees were hardened against accepting Jesus as Messiah. Who can accept the joy of the new under such a staggering burden?

Yet Jesus tells us in Matthew 18:3–4 that unless we become like little children, we will never enter the kingdom of heaven. What child would tarry under an eight-hundred-page weight? And our Lord says, *Whoever humbles himself like this child is the greatest in the kingdom of heaven* (ESV).

After the trampoline, I began to wonder what that might look like. How do I come to Jesus like a child?

❧   ❧   ❧

When I make that promise to play, I make the mistake of telling my children. And they hold me to it. Play to them usually means going out of doors. It is something they just do—quite like breathing. So we enter into the promise together—my two growing boys and I—and I am taken by surprise at the sudden depth of longing it awakens in me.

Every evening we go outside. After dinner, we take our dog—Lucy Mae—and we stroll leisurely down to the creek. The slow moving has a way of opening my eyes. There is no destination, just a savoring of time together under the canopy of open sky. This deliberate slowing has a way of stretching me—growing me. In the confines of my grown-up life, I have forgotten this feeling—this wonder and freedom that comes with no walls. In my grown-up life, when I want to grow or learn, I pick up a book. This is quite satisfying and I am happy this way—but after a time of stepping into the promise, I begin to remember.

It reminds me of childhood, this feeling.

When I was a little girl, each day would unfold in exquisite spontaneity—each dawning ripe with untapped possibility, each moment standing alone in its potential for adventure. At some unknown point on the ticking clock, my sister would look at me and utter the inevitable. *Let's play outside.* Those simple words were an invitation into a new land.

Outside, we were explorers on highly sensitive expeditions, adventurers conquering foreign territories. The discovery of something new was as close as the next hillcrest. Every inch of the land surrounding our childhood home held a singular fascination. Sometimes it feels like that sense of adventure in me—that wonder about the world—is gone forever. Little bits of it peek into my life from time to time, and I startle in recognition. I wonder if I imagined all those adventures . . . if they simply ceased to be because my grown-up mind has lost the ability to play this way.

Let's play outside.

What I didn't realize then is that those adventures were a way of tasting God—*of falling in love with God.* Looking back, I see his companionship in those moments of innocent curiosity. He walked with me through the woods surrounding my home. He flew through the air with me when I was airborne off a bike ramp. He wondered at the feathery softness of the milkweed with me. When I was a child, life was so *wonder-full.* The wonder of God's beautiful world was expanding my heart—making room for him who is wonderful to take up residence there—carving the perfect place inside of me that only he could fill.

But to find this wonder, *I had to step outside.*

Isn't it the same in my grown-up life? To chase the God-bliss, do I dare to *step outside* of my preconceived notions of what a mature spiritual life looks like? Do I shed some of the self-imposed rules I subscribe to—not worry about what others might think?

To find the God-joy, I have to be like David when the Ark of the Covenant is brought to Jerusalem. In 2 Samuel 6:14–15, Scripture tells us, "David, wearing a linen ephod, danced before the LORD with all his might, while he and the entire house of Israel brought up the ark of the LORD with shouts and the sound of trumpets" (NIV 1984).

And though he was ridiculed and despised by his wife for what she saw as behavior unworthy of a king, David refused to apologize. "I will celebrate before the LORD," he said. "I will become even more undignified than this, and I will be humiliated in my own eyes" (2 Sam. 6:21–22 NIV 1984).

He refused to let another person define what type of behavior was acceptable. Am I willing to become *even more undignified*? Am I willing to be *humiliated in my own eyes* and the eyes of my peers to deepen my relationship with God? Will I let go of what others define as "proper" behavior? Trusting God fully—with childlike faith—may lead others to think me childish. But when my heart is engaged in worship with little thought of appearances—like a child who is not burdened by self-consciousness—then, like David, I am freed to experience the joy of the Lord. What others might see as time wasted, I know to be an investment in the life-giving, eternal love relationship only available with One Person.

Just like any relationship, growing close to God—finding the comfort level that banishes self-consciousness—takes spending time. Time alone—together.

So we play—just the two of us. What do you think of when I say "play"? My play looks different these days. We might take in a mid-afternoon concert at the library or peruse an art exhibit. Sometimes we run together, paint, create, or just curl up with a book under a shade tree. But it is when I am out of doors that I feel his constancy in sharp relief to my short memory and waning attention. How can I forget this? These moments when I attend to God are the moments that color returns back into life and my breath is deep and sure.

When I bend to look through flowing water—watch light play on sinuous arcs rippling over hidden life—I feel the liquefied parts of me pulled deep into the earth, to the beginning of time when Spirit hovered over sea.

When I stir earth—dig into her musty skin—her kin in me is stirred. I feel my dusty roots.

And when I lay back on the grass-bed and stare into an ocean of sky . . . I see the endless beauty of creation—of me and what I was created to be.

When I play outside, I commune with God. And while book-reading is good, and it whets my appetite for him, the play-dates? They energize. They captivate. Meeting with God in this way brings me in touch with a place inside of me that I had forgotten. Purposefully stepping out to meet God in this way ignites an otherworldly passion. It is about more than falling in love.

It's about staying in love.

iii

seesaw

when you can't find the rhythm

It was the first time he ever held my hand. We stood
under the stars on the bank of the lake beside his childhood home,
and he told me how, in high school, he used to mow the grass
around this tiny bed of water. It was his first job. I was breathless
from the pressure of his hand on mine—from the cool of night
clinging to my skin, from the warmth of the memories he gave
to me—and he said something I will never forget.

"I've made a list of things we're going to do together," he said.

And he made it clear this was a very long list—one that might
take a lifetime to accomplish.

I found this wildly romantic, of course, and to this day if the
coals of our relationship begin to cool, all I need to do is ask my
husband, "What's the next item on the list?" With that question,

we are back on the banks of the lake. We are young again, and all at once we are remembering who we are and dreaming of who we will become. The ember is kindled back to flame.

It's difficult enough tending the fire with this flesh-and-blood man—the one I kiss good-bye each morning, the one I sleep beside every night and whose arms I seek in joy and sorrow. I can touch him, look into his eyes, feel the heat of his breath on my cheek . . . and still there are times when he feels far away from me. How do I do this with God? How do I maintain intimacy with an invisible being whose very existence requires seeing with eyes of faith? The question opens my heart to such a deep longing that there seems no way to the bottom of it.

I used to think the answer was found in the making of lists. I had a life plan. A list of goals.

I finished school (education—check), found a cool job (career—check), got married (relationship—check), bought a house (stability—check), started going to church (moral fiber—check), and had a couple of kids (family—check). I thought I was on my way to completion—to filling that void that gnawed aching into my inward parts. But every time I marked something off the list . . . the next thing arose to take its place. It became an endless list—an insurmountable mountain of checkmarks towering over this desperate heart.

But I was okay with the list—isn't this the way of life? Set the goal and then go for it. Check it off the list. This growing collection of checkmarks in my pocket . . . it felt . . . good. I was achieving something. I was making it. I was in control.

After I had children, I tried even harder at the list. The big list became lots of little ones. I invested myself in the church life. First it was the nursery (check), then the toddler's story time (check), then teaching Sunday school to the elementary-aged kids (check, check)—my spiritual life grew with my two boys. I joined a women's group and started Bible study and kept a morning quiet time (check). And it seemed to work just fine. For a time.

I made friends in Bible study that I know I will have for life—women who have loved me through the ugly and the beautiful. Their deep-root love enabled me to grow in ways I never imagined possible. In the safety of their fold, I learned much about God's Word and, too, during this time, found the joy in keeping spiritual disciplines—regular prayer and study. I was blissfully happy.

But as I grew, something terribly wonderful began to happen: everything changed. It felt like I woke up one morning and my God-life turned topsy-turvy. What was once deeply rewarding began to feel like skimming the surface of his love. The spiritual practices that once fed me became hollow and rote.

The list failed me. Life felt like a giant teeter-totter—alternating between the highs of my list-checking victories and the lows of realizing these accomplishments left me empty inside.

See, the trouble with lists is that sometimes—in the checking off of the items—I lose track of the meaning. The finishing of the list becomes the focus. It doesn't take long for me to forget the reasons I started the list. The items or events on the list are diminished—they become simply another item to complete. I lose the hope of a rich experience in the doing. I lose the power of recognizing God in each action. When the list becomes my anchor, I am making it a god. I am doing what Scripture tells me not to do—I am making an idol.

And I am no better than a Pharisee with my eight hundred pages of rules.

That list my husband made? The one of all the things we will do together? The beauty of that list is that it leads me to a place of expectation about the future with my man while—at the same time—prompting me to look back at the beginning of our relationship. It helps me remember all the wonderful, beautiful, difficult places we've been together.

Doesn't God want this, too? Doesn't he want us to look back and remember all the times he has walked with us—carried us—through the seasons of life? He frequently tells his people *to remember.* Not only does he repeatedly tell his people to *remember,* he tells them to create physical reminders to help the remembering. Outward signs to prompt inward changes.

> These commandments that I give you today are to be
> on your hearts. Impress them on your children. Talk
> about them when you sit at home and when you walk
> along the road, when you lie down and when you get
> up. Tie them as symbols on your hands and bind them
> on your foreheads. Write them on the doorframes of
> your houses and on your gates. (Deut. 6:6–9)

When Joshua led the Israelites through the Jordan River—when God stopped the flow of water and allowed them to walk across on dry ground—God told them to leave stones in the place as a visual sign of remembrance.

> And Joshua set up at Gilgal the twelve stones they had
> taken out of the Jordan. He said to the Israelites, "In

the future when your descendants ask their parents,
'What do these stones mean?' tell them, 'Israel crossed
the Jordan on dry ground.' For the LORD your God
dried up the Jordan before you until you had crossed
over. The LORD your God did to the Jordan what he
had done to the Red Sea when he dried it up before us
until we had crossed over. He did this so that all the
peoples of the earth might know that the hand of the
LORD is powerful and so that you might always fear the
LORD your God." (Josh. 4:20–24)

Scripture gives example after example of the Lord calling his
people to remember. He knows. He knows our tendency to forget.
And he knows the power in remembering. When I idolize the list,
I don't remember. I don't remember God's faithfulness. My eyes
are too busy scanning to the next item on the list.

That famous love doctor, John Gottman, PhD, knows the
power of remembering, too. For decades, Dr. Gottman has studied what makes marriages successful. He has what he calls the
Love Lab. It's a place—a studio apartment—set up to observe
couples and the ways they interact. In his book, *The Seven
Principles for Making Marriage Work*, Dr. Gottman asserts that
after years of research, he can predict with 91 percent accuracy
which couples will stay married. What's more, he says he can do
this after observing the couples interact in the Love Lab for only
five minutes.

One of the things he has found to impact a couple's chances
of staying married is the way they remember. In happy marriages, when couples look back, they tend to remember the high

points—the happy times. Unhappy couples tend to rewrite the past—emphasizing the bad memories or not remembering at all. When Dr. Gottman asks a couple to recount their wedding day—or the way they met, or their courtship, or anything really—the way they tell their story tells him a lot about what their future may hold.

Remembering well is important in relationships. It's important in my relationship with God, too.

But my lists don't encourage remembering. As soon as I check an item off . . . it's gone. I forget. When I move through my lists in a state of forgetfulness, it becomes less about what God can do and more about me. About what I can do. And I am tempted to hold that list up as evidence of my greatness. It becomes an idol.

When I make an idol of the list, not only do I forget what God has done *for* me, but I stop dreaming about what he wants to do *through* me.

When the Lord first spoke to Abraham to call him into relationship, God said:

> Leave your country, your people and your father's
> household and go to the land I will show you. I will
> make you into a great nation and I will bless you; I will
> make your name great, and you will be a blessing. I
> will bless those who bless you, and whoever curses you
> I will curse; and all peoples on earth will be blessed
> through you. (Gen. 12:1–3 NIV 1984)

Hebrews 11—that great Hall of Faith—tells us that Abraham obeyed and went by faith, *even though he did not know where he was going* (verse 8).

I wonder where we would be now if, when God called Abraham, our good father had said, "I'm sorry, Lord. I've got things to do. I have a list. Besides, until you tell me *exactly* how you're going to do this thing, I'm not sure I want to be involved. My way might be better."

Isn't this what I do every day? I ask for evidence. I ask for proof that his plan is better than mine. And when I stick with my plan—my list—don't I close the door to the many blessings God has for me? Lists are not play. The truth is, when my eye is on the list, I fail to see the wonder all around me—the beauty that God has given in each moment. It's like having spiritual blinders.

But this is what I did. I made lists. Lists of what needed doing in any given day. Lists of what to make for dinner. Lists of days of the week and what to do on each one. On Tuesdays and Fridays, I cleaned the bathrooms. On Monday nights, we had lasagna. On work nights, certain chores were done. On weekends, others. Life became a flurry of little lists. And all the while the deep soul yearning churned in the soil of my heart, unearthing restlessness and discontent in my inner life. The more established I grew, the more insistent the longing became.

No matter how many lists I made, I couldn't get to the bottom of the emptiness. Sometimes? Sometimes the lists made the ache stand out in sharp relief. There was the evidence, all written down, of all that I have done, and still . . . still the insatiable craving for more.

I recognize this and yet—I still make lists. There are days when the stuff of life presses in on me so close that I can't lift my head without gasping for air. The lists help me lope along on those days. So, here's the question: How do I make a list that helps me remember but also lets me dream? Is there a way to marry the legalism of the list-making with God's command to remember?

Because the days I am happiest? When I feel closest to God? Those are the days I throw the lists away. So, here's the deal. If you want to be productive, let the lists lead. But if you want to get closer to God?

Remember.

iv

bird-watching

the joy of beginnings

This morning, at my feeder: a rose-breasted gros-beak. It is early spring and the regulars have come—the gold-finches still wearing their dull-green winter feathers, the sparrows and cardinals, my spritely chickadees and titmice. But this black-hooded visitor with his blushing breast has me beside myself with delight. I've never seen one—not live and in feather. Later, I will learn why. The Cornell Lab of Ornithology website tells me he prefers the woodlands to the suburbs, and he commonly habitats a wee bit more northerly than my West Virginia valley home, fanning up into southeastern and central Canada. The color-coded map tells me that he sometimes breeds here, but more than likely he is only passing through—returning to his northern home from a winter stay in southern Mexico or Central

America. I peek timidly from the side of the window, watching this beauty pick my sunflower seeds with his conical bill, afraid if I move he might startle away.

I could stand this way for endless moments, memorizing his every feature and longing to be gifted with a note or two of his song. I slip to the cupboard and pull out my field guide. I scan the description for telltale markings, noting that this bird has no "prominent white eyebrow"—indicating my visitor is, indeed, male. I hover by the window, unnoticed—a ghost who is falling in love.

My dictionary defines the word *rapture* as "ecstatic joy or delight" and "the carrying of a person to another place or sphere of existence."[1] This is where I am as I watch the grosbeak. Raptured.

In her memoir *An American Childhood*, Annie Dillard says this about bird-watching: "The tizzy that birds excite in the beginner are a property of the beginner, not of the birds; so those who love the tizzy itself must ever keep beginning things" (220).

The nineteenth-century French writer Stendhal calls this infatuation with beginnings *crystallization*. In his essay *L'Amour* (Love), he describes how he arrived at such terminology: "At the salt mines of Salzburg, they throw a leafless wintry bough into one of the abandoned workings. Two or three months later they haul it out covered with a shining deposit of crystals. The smallest twig . . . is studded with a galaxy of scintillating diamonds. The original branch is no longer recognizable" (45).

Stendhal says this is the perfect picture of how our minds look when we fall in love. Our unconscious begins, as David Brooks puts it in his book *The Social Animal*, to "coat the objects of our love with shimmering and irresistible light" (205).

Do you remember when you first fell in love? Experts tell us that the early stages of romantic love are like nothing else—our every thought is for the beloved. And after each foray into daydream, we emerge with an image of the loved one that sparkles ever more brilliantly in the light of our affection. It's a time of deep awakening when every sense is attuned to beauty and—as Stendhal illustrates—our eye seeks out only that which affirms the remarkable nature of our sweetheart.

It is, as the pop psychologists say, a happy place. A place of rapture.

When you fell in love with Jesus, was it much the same? Did you spend countless hours poring over Scripture? Did sleep suddenly seem mundane as you rose before dawn each day to meet with him? Was every sunset an expression of his love? And did every sermon hold a secret message just for you?

Isn't this the place we all long to return to in our spiritual lives? We hunger for the sweet place that will be unhindered by the daily grind of life. We all long for the bliss of an intimate, unrestrained love relationship with God.

But how can we return? Just as any relationship can settle into the ordinary, so might our relationship with God lose this sense of wonder so palpable in the new. How do we get back those diamond lenses of crystallization—that euphoric love of beginnings in our God-life? Is it even possible in our human relationships—let alone in our relationship with God?

Researchers Bianca Acevedo, Arthur Aron, Helen Fisher, and Lucy Brown think so, as noted in *Social Cognitive and Affective Neuroscience*. They compared functional Magnetic Resonance Imaging (fMRI) brain scans of individuals who had recently fallen in love to those of happily married couples who reported intense romantic love for their partner after an average of twenty-one years of marriage.

The scans were remarkably similar—showing the same activity in areas of the brain associated with the reward center. These areas of the brain are typically associated with motivation and are rich in dopamine—a chemical in the brain that is known to cause feelings of euphoria or pleasure. This tells us that, even after twenty-one years of marriage, thoughts of the loved one ignite a deep satisfaction—fill a deep craving. (This is the area of the brain that also lights up on the fMRI scans of addicts when they take cocaine.) But, unlike those of the newly in love, the long-in-love brains show no activity in areas associated with anxiety and fear. Instead, they show activation in brain regions that are associated with maternal love, or bonding. This doesn't mean people want to parent their partners—just that strong attachments are present . . . one might even say joy.

The excitement of new love and the security of old love all twined together, bound to each other in a shimmering ribbon of beauty.

But researchers admit these individuals who are able to hold on to passion over the slow passing of seasons are the exception, not the norm. Most studies confirm the steady decline of romantic love over time—that hot glow of passion burns into the slow ember of companionate love. So what is different about these long-term lovers that enables them to hold on to that knee-buckling quality of new love?

Researcher Arthur Aron has a theory. Dr. Aron has been studying love in its varying forms since the 1970s. One early study he co-authored—termed the "bridge study"—suggested a link between arousal and attraction (Dutton and Aron). In the study, male subjects rated a woman as more attractive when they encountered her on a scary suspension bridge than when they met the same woman on a stationary foot bridge. Could this be a key to maintaining excitement in a love relationship?

This understanding of the relationship between arousal and attraction, combined with later research, led Dr. Aron and his wife, Elaine—also a researcher—to propose the self-expansion model of love. This model suggests that "when people love, they are at least sometimes, in some sense, seeking an infinitely expanding self."

In an article published in the journal *Personal Relationships* in 1996, Aron and Aron elaborate:

> [P]eople seek to expand not only their physical
> influence (through territoriality, power relationships,
> possessions, etc.), but also their cognitive complexity
> (knowledge, insight), their social and bodily identity
> (by including as part of themselves other individuals,
> whole groups such as family or nation, and nonhumans
> ranging from animals to gods), and their awareness
> of their position in the universe (that unique human
> interest in metaphysics, the meaning of life, ritual,
> religion, mythology, etc.). (47)

In other words, we tend to seek out ways and relationships in life that will help us grow. And when we fall in love, we expand our view of ourselves to include qualities, interests, and experiences that our beloved possesses. In this way, we see ourselves as more interesting and more exciting, and we feel the challenge of learning about new things. The Arons call this *self-expansion*. They define a self-expanding activity as any activity that is arousing or novel.

The self-expansion model speculates that the excitement usually experienced in the early stages of a relationship is related to rapid development of closeness. When a relationship begins to bloom, there is much for the partners to discover and learn about each other. Over time, as a couple gets to know each other better, excitement slows down and levels off. But, if partners continue to pursue exciting activities together (any activity seen as novel), passion can be reignited through the association of excitement with the relationship. The Arons' research indicates that long-term marital satisfaction and romantic love is maintained when partners engage in self-expanding experiences together.

So, if you feel your partner is helping you grow into a better, more interesting person, then you will be more satisfied and report more excitement in the relationship.

But what does this mean in our God-relationship? Do I need to meet God on a rickety bridge to reignite my passion for him?

I am comparing my human love relationships to my relationship with God, and here I want to pause and observe caution. When I apply my limited human perspective to the Infinite, I run the risk of making God too small. It was Zophar the Naamathite— that ancient philosopher and "helper" of Job—who asks, "Canst thou by searching find out God? Canst thou find out the Almighty unto perfection?" (Job 11:7 KJV). My *New International Version* puts it this way: "Can you fathom the mysteries of God? Can you probe the limits of the Almighty?" Zophar may have been wrong about many things that day, but here he gives us wisdom. There is no way I will ever figure out God. All that I know of him—it comes from him. Whether through Scripture, or nature, or studying the life of Jesus, or through the divine revelation of the Holy Spirit—I only know what he chooses to reveal. Scripture tells me that this is only *part* of the story (1 Cor. 13:12).

This is what spiritual practices do for me. They help keep my mind tuned to the divine, the unseen. For example, each time I approach God in my home, I light a candle. God doesn't need that candle to meet with me. But I do. Every time my mind gets distracted, all I need to do is glance at that flickering flame, and I am reminded that I am not alone. It is because of my own weakness that I seek out ways to bring my mind and heart into an awareness that there is more to this world than what my eyes can see. God is so much more than I can understand.

And yet, James 4:8 tells me, "Come near to God and he will come near to you." This is what I am doing when I seek out a playdate with my Lord. I sidle up to him, drawing ever nearer, each time I deliberately invite him into my day. In this way, I remember that *God is a person*, even if I cannot understand all there is to know about him. And just as with all people, the best way to grow in relationship is to spend time together.

What self-expansion theory says is that time doing *new* things together is one way to maintain—or recover—the excitement in our relationship. Ironically, it is this contradiction of character traits in God—he is the transcendent God who is, at the same time, deeply personal—that make self-expansion theory so exciting to apply to our God-lives. If God is infinite—greater in every way I can imagine—and if I seek to expand myself by incorporating what I know of him into my character . . . the possibilities are endless. This is what we mean by sanctification, is it not? God is continually calling us to new life, and we become more and more like Jesus as we grow in faith. Romans 8:29 says, "For those God foreknew he also predestined to be conformed to the image of his Son, that he might be the firstborn among many brothers and sisters." Christ's character is continually being infused in me as I expand my view of myself to include his perfect righteousness.

This idea of novel activities enhancing our perception of the way the moments pass is supported by other research as well. People who have studied time know this to be true. They say that time seems to move slower when I am not paying attention to the ticking hand—when I am participating in activities that are new and require my full attention.

And don't I know this? The days break and run and I crane my neck as they pass—sometimes all I feel is the afterbreeze of a moment gone by. They tell me it means I'm getting old, and I always laugh and agree. I thought it was just a tease . . . but science is telling me different.

"Time is this rubbery thing," says neuroscience professor David Eagleman in an interview with *New Yorker* journalist Burkhard Bilger. "It stretches out when you really turn your brain resources on, and when you say, 'Oh, I got this, everything is as expected,' it shrinks up." Emotion and memory are housed in the part of the brain called the amygdala, he explains. When we are excited by something out of the ordinary—like a threat to one's life—the amygdala seems to become hypersensitive, picking up every tiny detail experienced. The more attention to detail, the longer the moment seems to last. "This explains why we think that time speeds up when we grow older," Eagleman says.[2] So that's why time after forty seems to increase in speed exponentially as we look back longingly to those long summers of our youth. As the world becomes more familiar, our brains get lazy and attend to less information. And the days seem to slip through our fingers like the ocean.

Every day dawns familiar. I miss the little bits of beauty dropped into my life—because my amygdala has been lulled to sleep. So I do the only thing I can to slow the moments.

I look for adventure in my every day. If every day is, well . . . everyday—then shouldn't I?

When my spirit grows tired and my heart drags on the ground behind—isn't it only natural to seek adventure? For me it is. God takes my hand and we go. Because he knows what the scientists keep trying to prove.

Every moment is sacred when we pay attention to it.

Adam Galinsky, professor at the Kellogg School of Management at Northwestern University, says getting away from the familiar gives one the distance needed to "gain a new perspective on everyday life." He even has evidence that immersing oneself in another culture—moving to another country—boosts creativity (Hamilton).

Seeking out the new. With a holy God. Am I crazy?

With God, I don't need to travel abroad. He takes me to new, heart-molding, mind-boggling places when I open up my heart to him. When I step out in faith—when I go to a new place, try a new activity, see something old with new eyes—time is savored.

And it stretches long.

It's not another culture, but it's different to me. I pray for new eyes. I pray for *God-eyes*. We walk the streets together; my senses awaken to the new in the familiar. Time moves slow. And love is young again. I am a child awakening once more to the wonder of the world around me. And I look at my Beloved through the dewy lens of crystallization.

If I am to find the tizzy, as Annie Dillard says, I must keep seeking out beginnings. Jesus said it best—*we must become like little children*. He knew this is the way to capture the joy of beginnings. For—to a child—all the world is a beginning; all the world is new.

Notes

¹ *Dictionary.com*, definition of rapture, accessed October 20, 2012, http://dictionary.reference.com/browse/rapture.

² Burkhard Bilger, "The Possibilian," *New Yorker*, April 25, 2011, www. newyorker.com/reporting/2011/04/25/110425fa_fact_bilger.

V

God's suitcase

the wild joy of wonder

An instructor in a class I recently attended told the story of a six-year-old boy who was moving across the country with his family. They stopped to visit with this good teacher, who is a friend of the family. When time came to leave, this young fellow expressed his sorrow to depart from his kind friend. He thought she might like to come along. Maybe in his suitcase. When his mother suggested this dear woman might not fit in such a confining space, he said, "But she could fit in God's suitcase. God's suitcase is big enough to fit anything."

I wonder when I stopped believing that with God all things are possible.

Perhaps "stopped believing" is too harsh a phrase. For, if you ask me directly, I will tell you that God can do anything. But I wonder . . . when did my imagination become so small that I stopped expecting the seemingly impossible? When did my feet become so rooted to the crust of the earth that I let gravity weigh down my idea of who God is?

If I asked psychologist Jean Piaget that question, he would tell me that my ideas about God and about this world probably drastically shrunk in size around age seven or eight.

I don't remember much about seven, do you? That season of childhood flits in and out of consciousness like scenes from an old movie—cast in an amber glow of mystery. I was in second grade at age seven—smitten with horses and Barbie dolls. I remember sitting in Mrs. Southern's classroom and daydreaming that Fonzi or the Six Million Dollar Man would jump through the window and carry me away. My brothers and sister and I had a kind of folklore all our own—stories about the hills surrounding our hollow and its history. We named favorite places according to these fables—The Indian Road, The Muddy Hideout, The Black Spot. We told stories of how—at dusk—the animals would transform and talk to each other of deep, secret things.

According to Jean Piaget's theory of cognitive development, a child of age seven is in the preoperational stage of thought. WebMD (one of those glorious online places I go to define all things related to the human body) says this stage spans ages two through seven and is characterized by the development of the ability to think symbolically (Benaroch). Young children also develop memory and imagination at this stage, which allows the engagement in rich make-believe play.

The WebMD writers tell me that one "limitation" of preoperational thinking is that it is based on intuition instead of logic.

This makes it difficult to grasp cause and effect, time, and comparison. Intuition is defined by most dictionaries as an insight into truth that is not perceived by the conscious mind. But I like to think of it as that place where the Holy Spirit touches my consciousness—steering me this way or that. Indeed, it might be seen as a limitation by the world when we make decisions based merely on internal promptings . . . but I wonder . . . is it? Really? As Christians, shouldn't we be seeking out ways that make this Voice more discernible?

When a child advances into the next stage of cognitive development—the concrete operational stage—from ages seven through twelve, logic and concrete reasoning take over. These kids aren't nearly as fun to talk to as their younger, more intuitive, counterparts.

Overheard in the preschool room on Sunday:

"I'm a princess, see? I have this crown."

She walks about the circle of boys and girls majestically.

"Oh, no!" says a freckle-faced boy from a distant corner of the princess's kingdom. "The dragon wants your crown!"

He takes the stuffed dragon he's been cradling in his lap and attacks the princess's head.

Two warrior-girls step in, wearing butterfly wings on their backs.

"We'll save you," cries one. "Come with us up to the cloud castle!"

They scoop her arms in theirs and fly away.

When we abandon the trappings of logic, not only does the world become bigger ... God does, too. When we admit there are things that we cannot understand, we give our minds permission to open to the sheer magnitude of all that God is capable of. In her book *Mindfulness*, psychologist and researcher Ellen J. Langer quotes the mathematician Henri Poincarè: "It is by logic that we prove. It is by intuition that we discover" (116).

I want to discover more of God, don't you?

In the grown-up world, if I am to believe God the way a little child does, it is implied that I must employ *suspension of disbelief*—a term first used by the poet Samuel Taylor Coleridge in 1817 in his work *Biographia Literaria*. In an attempt to recapture the imagination of a world held captive by the new science of the industrial revolution, Coleridge reintroduced fantastical elements into poetry—writing of visions and beings from the spiritual realm that had long been abandoned in favor of more practical imagery. Suspension of disbelief implies that to go along with a storyline, I should ignore certain aspects of the plot that are seemingly impossible. In this way, I look over what I know to be true—what my eye sees—into the greater narrative of the story.

Coleridge says, in chapter XIV of *Biographia Literaria*:

> It was agreed, that my endeavours should be directed
> to persons and characters supernatural, or at least
> romantic, yet so as to transfer from our inward nature
> a human interest and a *semblance of truth* [emphasis
> mine] sufficient to procure for these shadows of
> imagination that willing suspension of disbelief for the
> moment, which constitutes poetic faith. (99)

A *semblance of truth.*

This may sit well with poetry, but in the realm of faith, isn't this backwards? When Jesus said, "Truly I tell you, anyone who will not receive the kingdom of God like a little child will never enter it," (Mark 10:15) I don't think he was telling us to *suspend disbelief.* Maybe, instead of suspending disbelief, we need to practice *expansion of belief.*

Isn't this the way of a little child? To open the mind wide enough that the huge presence of the impossible can fit inside? Children don't *suspend disbelief.* They enter into belief with the whole of their being. So it becomes true that animals do talk. Ancient peoples leave messages for us on dirt roads and tree bark. God invites us over for tea parties. And grown-ups really can fit into suitcases.

In her 2012 release, *Still: Notes on a Mid-Faith Crisis,* author Lauren Winner describes a 1967 research article she read that was designed to study how a child's view of prayer transforms over the years. In it, the researchers concluded that "children's ideas about prayer don't just change—they develop; they progress from less sophisticated to more sophisticated" (76).

The authors of the study observe that children's ideas of prayer become more abstract as they age. As Winner quotes:

> [T]he four-year-old's notion that "a prayer is about
> God, rabbits . . . and deer, and Santa Claus and turkeys
> and pheasants, and Jesus and Mary and Mary's little
> baby" becomes, at seven, "prayer is when you ask for
> something you need, like water or rain or snow," and
> then at twelve, the child begins to speak theologically:

prayer is how you communicate with God, how you ask
God for forgiveness. . . . (76)

As Winner reads on, she realizes the authors' statement about
the older child understanding that he or she is "the author of his
own prayers" doesn't necessarily reflect an advance in thought
development. She writes:

> But I do not think it is an advance. I think it is
> something those children will unlearn, later, if they
> keep praying. I think they will come to know that the
> youngest children are right. I think they will come
> to know that their prayers do not, in fact come from
> within themselves. I can participate in prayer (or not),
> show up to pray (or not), but I am not the author of my
> prayers; when they come, they come from God. (77)

I wonder if—when our brains reach that magical time for the
capability of logic—the wonder structures in our neuroanatomy
have to shrink to make room? And . . . is there a way in the
grown-up world to clean out the closets of our minds and make
room for wonder again?

Ellen J. Langer suggests that one reason we can become
narrow-minded in this way is our tendency to focus on outcomes.

> When children start a new activity with an outcome ori-
> entation, questions of "Can I?" or "What if I can't do it?"
> are likely to predominate, creating an anxious preoccu-
> pation with success or failure rather than drawing on
> the child's natural, exuberant desire to explore. Instead
> of enjoying the color of the crayon, the designs on the

paper, and a variety of possible shapes along the way, the child sets about writing a "correct" letter A. (34)

Don't I—as an adult—focus on outcome above all? I look around and compare my achievements with my peers, and instead of enjoying the journey, it becomes about who has the most successful career, the nicest house, the best-behaved children, or the most disciplined prayer time. When I play that comparison game, the intrinsic, *unseen* rewards will lose out every time. It's the to-do list all over again. Do you remember what we said about preoperational thought and comparison?

Because it's based on intuition instead of logic, preoperational thinking *makes it difficult to grasp cause and effect, time, and comparison.* And while it would be irresponsible to throw these cognitive tools completely out the window, wouldn't most adults benefit from the ability to step outside of these places of logic and open themselves up to possibility—at least some of the time?

How can a grown-up recover the wild joy of wonder?

The answer came on the trampoline that cold day in February—lifted with laughter on the snow.

Play.

In his book *Play: How It Shapes the Brain, Opens the Imagination, and Invigorates the Soul,* Dr. Stuart Brown says there is enough anecdotal evidence to conclude that when play is a regular part of our lives, our brains work better.

Brown cites studies by play researcher Jaak Panksepp on the advantages of play: "[A]ctive play selectively stimulates brain-derived neurotrophic factor (which stimulates nerve growth) in the amygdala (where emotions get processed) and the dorsolateral prefrontal cortex (where executive decisions are processed)" (33).

Brown also cites studies that show time spent in play is related to the development of the brain's frontal cortex—the part of the brain responsible for sophisticated levels of thought processing such as planning and organizing information, anticipating outcomes of behaviors, and self-monitoring. The amount of play has been shown to affect the rate of growth and size of the cerebellum, as well. This brain structure has been found to be tied to crucial aspects of cognition such as attention and language processing.

Brown concludes that play activity helps *sculpt the brain*. Play makes us use more of our brains, stimulating greater growth and possibly promoting better overall functioning.

But adult play can look very different from child's play, can it not? What does grown-up play look like? And how do I know what activities will open my mind to wonder?

According to Dr. Brown, true play has seven characteristics:

1. Play is *apparently purposeless.* Play is something we do because we enjoy doing it. Not because it has any practical value.
2. Play is *voluntary.* There is no coercion or requirement to participate where play is concerned.
3. Play has *inherent attraction.* That means it's fun and exciting. Play is something you want to do.
4. Play gives a sense of *freedom from time.* When immersed in play activities, minutes flow smoothly and we lose track of their passing.

5. In play there is a *diminished consciousness of self.* We lose all sense of self-consciousness and live fully in the moment.

6. Play has *improvisational potential.* Play allows us to break out of old mindsets and opens us up to new ways of doing things.

7. Play provides *continuation desire.* It is something we want to keep doing. It gives us so much pleasure that we find ways to make sure we can do it again and again. (17–18)

I've never tried to define play in this way—only sought to enjoy it. Indeed, if I did try to operationalize it, the word "joy" would definitely be involved. In her book *The Gift of Play: Why Adult Women Stop Playing and How to Start Again*, author Barbara Brannen calls play that contains an element of joy "heart play." She distinguishes joy from fun.

> Fun is not bad, it is better than nothing, but let us be clear early on that fun is very different from joy.
>
> Joy is the ability to feel your heart sing. The ability for you to feel so good that you absolutely cannot stop grinning. The ability to feel warm all over. When you are through playing you are able to retrieve the experience from your memory bank and relive it. You are able to recapture the moment with joy all over again. When you think about your play you can focus on it and feel instantly refreshed. Your play opens your heart. When your heart is open you open your eyes and see things for what they really are.

> Your spirit is opened and you can feel everything
> to a greater degree. You are no longer numb to the
> world, but experiencing it fully and with great glee. (24)

For me, play has always been a way of opening up to intuition—that place where the Holy Spirit speaks more clearly into my heart. Play gives me permission to pay attention to this gentle prodding that I might otherwise ignore.

Recently, the way I have felt the power of play heighten my awareness of the Holy Spirit has been through running. Although I have been a runner off and on since adolescence, a few years ago this discipline took on new meaning in my spiritual life. Running had become a chore for my aging body—something I did for health benefits and to set a good example for my children. I no longer enjoyed the daily thrashing this putting one foot in front of the other seemed to unleash on my body; in fact, I had come to dread it.

Things changed when my family gave me a smart phone for Mother's Day in 2011. I downloaded an app that kept track of my mileage and used a GPS to map out my course. This allowed me to change up my route on a whim and still keep track of how far I'd gone. I began to explore our little valley on foot, discovering new hollows and roads I had not noticed before.

One evening, after a particularly long day at work and with flagging spirits, I was running up a hill I had crested many times. But on that particular night, the timing was just right for me to see the sky catch on fire with a spectacular sunset. I was blown away.

Without thinking, I snapped a picture with my phone. Later, I shared the image on Facebook. That one little action opened up a whole new dimension in my spiritual life. From that moment on, running became about looking for glimpses of beauty—opening my eyes to the ways the hands of God touch the earth. My eyes were opened to loveliness in the most unusual places—dilapidated barns and old fence posts, the way a naked tree frames the blue of the sky, the sun making shine on the water . . . it only takes a moment to point and shoot. Last summer, I snapped pictures of the wildflowers I encountered and learned all of their names. My running time became a prayer—a continuous conversation with God.

The images that God brought into clear focus often evoked a particular question, a memory, or simple wonder. Words began to form in response to the images and soon my runs became writing exercises, too.

In January, on an unseasonably warm day, a quick shot of the water reservoir brought this:

> *"It seems like you might be having an identity crisis," she*
> *said, as the sun made its glisten. "But don't worry . . .*
> *we've all been there. It makes the coming back around*
> *all the more beautiful."*

On a quiet, spare autumn evening:

> *"How brave you are," she said, "to show your true*
> *underneath. Is it scary to stand so tall and bare like*
> *that? Does it hurt?"*

> *But the tree just hushed her with close rubbing branches.*

On a hot, August day when I ran up on the stump of a burned-out tree:

> *So many days the ashes seemed to rise up to meet her,*
> *but if she looked close . . . there was always something*
> *growing underneath.*

These little snippets became messages from God for me—wisdom to frame my life. A friend helped me set up a Facebook page so others could join me in sharing what God spoke during these playtimes. The page has never had a huge following . . . and that's okay. Because the goal is not to drive traffic, but to let these captured moments be the flint that sparks a deeper look at this beautiful world God has given to us.

Seeing the old with new eyes. Letting intuition lead me closer into God's embrace. These things take our hearts back in time to that place where trust was as natural as breathing. It requires a strong faith to forget the cares of the world and trust that Jesus will take care of our needs. This kind of childlike trust reminds me of the story of the sisters Mary and Martha. In Luke 10, we see Martha making preparations to receive Jesus and his disciples as guests in her home. But Mary sits at his feet and listens. When Martha complains to Jesus that her sister is not helping her, he tells her that Mary is doing the better thing. He says only "one thing" is needed. So many times I let grown-up distractions lead me away from sitting with him. It's a lack of trust that leads me to believe that only I can handle the details of the daily hassles. Can I not trust that if I draw near to him he will take care of the rest?

Could it be that coming to Jesus like a little child means more than expanding our belief—opening our eyes to wonder?

What if . . . what if Jesus gave us the image of children because they are so utterly dependent on their parents? Families looked a lot different in Jesus' time. Children were not the center of their parents' universe as they are today. Life was difficult, and adding another mouth to feed meant more work for everyone. Until they reached a certain age, children were unable to contribute anything to help with the work that went into feeding the family. But one thing they did very well: opening the empty hand. Children are excellent receivers.

Have you ever known a child to hide her need? Go to any favorite preschool destination, and what will you hear? *I'm hungry, Mommy. I'm firsty. I need a dwink of water, Daddy. Carry me, Daddy. Daddy? Mommy? MommyMommyMommyMomDad?*

Children are very skilled at expressing their needs. But here I stand with my fists clenched tightly, trying to prove to the world that there is nothing I need. I can take care of myself, see? I've got it all together. Maybe to become like a child means to hunger. To thirst. To stand naked in front of God and the world with all my needs. How I need grace. Love. Mercy. Forgiveness. My insides gnaw for justice. And kindness. Peace . . . anyone? Oh, Lord, I need beauty. Without beauty in my day, it feels like I am dying a slow death.

Do you remember the story in Luke 7 of the woman who washed Jesus' feet with her tears? She wiped them dry with her hair, kissing them over and over. The intimacy of such an action leaves a lump in my throat: *need.* Her need for Jesus took her to a place where she cared not what others thought.

I need Jesus that way, too.

This is the "one thing"—this need to be close to our Lord. I will sit at his feet with Mary. I will kiss his feet, empty out my alabaster jar. This is where it begins: on my knees, at his feet. Trusting that everything else will fall into place if I stay as close as I possibly can. That deeper intimacy will follow and my heart will be made young again.

Right now as I sit at my work station, I can see our neighbor's young children playing in their driveway. It's ninety degrees in the shade and they came outside early—in swimsuits. For hours all they have needed to ignite their imagination is a large orange bucket of water and some kind of spongy toy. I watch as they take turns dipping the sponge in the water and carrying it to various parts of the driveway, leaving a trail of water in their wake. They are soaked from head to foot and occasionally spin in place—flinging water as they go. Sometimes they forget themselves and drop the sponge to skip with abandon across the broad expanse of the drive.

My heart feels the pull of such simple play—such a careless way to whittle away the minutes of the day. I am thinking about packing them both up, along with the orange bucket, in God's suitcase.

I am thinking about making a quick getaway to the cloud castle.

vi

Super Soaker

when life feels dry

This morning I sit with the window open during my quiet time.

My mother-in-law stopped in during the praying, and I had to collect myself up off the floor to be social. It was a nice visit, but it doesn't take much to befuddle my prayers these days. When she left, I couldn't get it back. So I sit at the kitchen table with my Bible and a couple of commentaries—letting the cool spring air and the chatter of the finches wafting through the open window ease me back into that holy place. I'm trying to hear, but the Scriptures aren't speaking. Or maybe I'm not listening. I'm still thinking about that fuddled up prayer—wondering why I've had so much ADD lately.

For the past year, I've been working my way through a devotional book each morning. I read the Scripture assignments and journal my thoughts. As I journal, I pray out loud—dialogue with God about what's going on, inside and out. Trouble is, I finished the book. I thought I'd be glad to cross that milestone, but here I am . . . dangling. I don't want to start another devotional because I'm still digesting some of the things the other brought to light. So instead, I've been going straight to reading Scripture and writing down my thoughts. It's been so very sweet. But it feels so . . . loose.

It's liberating in a way. After all these weeks of such disciplined structure, my mind is a bit bouncy. I'm doing the random open-and-point-the-finger method. It's been fun to see where God takes me, but I know I need to be more focused. I'm thinking this when I notice the squirrel in my bird feeder. That rascal is stuffing his cheeks with every sunflower seed that will fit, and the rest he clumsily brushes out into the grass with his bushy tail. I feel my blood begin to boil. What about my little songbirds?

No worries, I've got this. Silently, I slip to the floor beside the open window. This is the other reason I have left it up. I discovered the perfect squirrel deterrent earlier this week—after numerous episodes of jumping up and running outside waving my arms like a maniac. I carefully pick up the water Uzi I have strategically placed under the sill, take aim, and fire. That squirrel doesn't know what hit him. He jumps three feet up and then down, runs across the yard, and disappears into the copse of hickory trees that seems to host an endless army of his kin.

For the better part of an hour, I lie on my belly just underneath the sill. Each time that fat squirrel makes his move . . . I make mine. Every time that squirrel jumps crazily into the air, I laugh so hard I can hardly get up off the floor—feeling the presence of God powerfully . . . laughing right along with me. Rather than letting what could have been an interruption frustrate me, I simply invite God into that moment. What a blast. Now I keep a water gun handy during my quiet time to chase squirrels away. Or other pesky creatures (like fourteen-year-olds).

It is one of the most refreshing not-so-quiet quiet times I've ever had. But do you know that until recently I wouldn't have dared share that story with my Christian girlfriends? Until recently, I would have worried they would think I was undisciplined in my Bible study, irresponsible, disrespectful, or just plain crazy. Grown-ups don't do things like that. Do they? Until recently, I don't think I would have allowed myself to fritter away a morning in such a way. What in the world would people think?

I've spent a lot of my life asking that question. Worrying what others would think, holding other women up as spiritual plumb lines, and somehow . . . somehow, I just never seem to measure up. Every other woman seems more dedicated to prayer, more disciplined in Bible study, more invested in service work, more generous to the poor, or a better provider for her household and family. Every other woman is that Proverbs 31 woman whose children rise up and call her blessed. And those children? They are probably well-mannered and never run out of clean underwear like mine.

I never seem to measure up. Have you ever felt that way?

❧　　　❧　　　❧

Last night, I dreamed I was walking through my neighborhood—this same old collection of streets and houses with manicured lawns and tidy landscaping that I have been walking for almost seventeen years now. In my dream, I discover a new street—a secret avenue that is shaded by long-growing trees and surrounded by loping hills. On the hills are old barns—empty and long-forgotten. Sun-washed clapboards strain against gravity and windows stand gaping like all-seeing eyes; shutters bang in the breeze.

These old barns leave me breathless with their tired beauty.

"How did I not know these are here?" I ask an unknown companion who is suddenly walking with me.

My fingers itch to photograph the quiet grace these barns speak to me. I walk in wonder, framing shots in my mind and fighting the urge to run home to collect my camera.

When I awaken, a question stirs inside me. I need to go and look. I need to see . . . to find the wonder that the dream evoked. At daybreak, I don my walking shoes and hit the streets. I know that I will not stumble upon a hidden passageway to the land of the beautiful barns, but I am looking for something. I'm not quite sure what, but when the sun breaks through a wisp of clouds on the horizon . . . there is beauty. These same old streets that I know by heart? I see them with new eyes.

As I wander under Bradford pears and consider symmetrical bushes of heather, I think about my neighbors and the love they have put into these familiar places that I pass unseeing every day.

Suddenly, the old is new.

Isn't this what Jesus does for us? Second Corinthians 5:17 says, "Therefore, if anyone is in Christ, he is a new creation. The old has passed away; behold, the new has come" (ESV).

I just need eyes to see. It's the search for the blue flower, the meeting on the rickety bridge, the expansion of belief . . . all these things and more come together when I see with God-eyes.

In his esteemed book *Prayer: Finding the Heart's True Home*, Richard J. Foster says, "The primary purpose of prayer is to bring us into such a life of communion with the Father that, by the power of the Spirit, we are increasingly conformed to the image of the Son" (57).

I think Richard Foster is familiar with Romans 8:29, which tells us: "For those God foreknew he also predestined to be conformed to the image of his Son, that he might be the firstborn among many brothers and sisters."

This is God's desire for us—that we might become like Jesus.

But what does this mean, "conformed to the image of the Son"?

It means to become similar—on the inside as well as the outside—for sure. But I wonder if it might mean something more? The word used in Romans 8 is transliterated *summorphos*, a Greek word that originates from *suvn* (phonetic *soon*)—a preposition that denotes union—and *morfhv* (phonetic *mor-fay'*), meaning external appearance. Conform.

I'm still thinking about conformity when, in mid-fall, I visit the apiary.

It all started when I spoke at a ladies' tea in a little country church in the valley where I live. The hostess served honey from her husband's hives, and I was blown away. "It tastes like sweet clover," I told her, as I sipped tea with my pinky raised. She smiled and nodded her head. This was entirely different from that syrupy stuff I buy in the bear-shaped bottle at the grocery.

Every day after that, I think about the bees. In the night, I dream of honey. When I awaken, I carry a memory of amber—a dewy sweetness on my tongue. I cannot shake the taste of it. So I Google local beekeepers, and I talk to the state bee inspector on the phone, and my father-in-law calls a friend of his who keeps bees.

"In the Bible, honey represents purity," the Department of Agriculture's state bee inspector tells me. "I think there must be bees in heaven," he says. I think about that little taste of honey from the tea, and it seems to me that maybe a little piece of heaven is already here.

I read all the Scriptures in my Bible about honey, and I look up the original Hebrew in my concordance. The word used for honey in many of the Scriptures refers to the distilled version of a watery sweetness that exists naturally. It is the *refined essence* of the substance—the richest part.

So. After weeks of waiting, when the goldenrods bend their heads low in the meadow behind my house, I visit the apiary. "That's how you know the goldenrod is nectaring," the beekeeper tells me. "The tops are so heavy they fall over."

We walk into the apiary under a shower of walnut tree leaves. They float slowly to the ground like tiny canoes, sailing the air. I breathe in deep, thinking of honey. The farm smells like woodsmoke and decaying leaves. The sky is blue marble.

I hear the steady thrum of thousands of beating wings rise into that familiar buzz while we are still within a hundred yards of the colonies. The sound thrills me, but I feel my heart begin to slow with the low resonance that emanates from the hives. The beekeeper aims his smoker at the bees flying about the first hive. I watch him open the tall, box-like structures and use his tools to remove one frame at a time. He lifts a frame and points out the shiny honey down in each little dimple of the wax.

The bees light haphazardly on my arms and midsection and on the veil I am wearing—they seem as curious about me as I am about them. I close my eyes and let the sound of their greeting fill the air—that low buzz pressing down around me. I know the smoke has made them docile, triggering them to consume as much honey as they can and slowing them down with the weight of it. They are afraid we have come to steal their golden treasure, and so they hide it the best way they know: inside their bulging abdomens.

He lets me take pictures of his bees, hunts out the queen for me to see. He is a good teacher—patient and kind. After he closes up the hives, he shows me his workshop. He makes beeswax candles and sells them. His wife has won numerous awards for baking with honey, and her blue ribbons hang on the wall by the door. He teaches candle making classes and gives talks about beekeeping.

He tells me about how the honeybees make honey—this refining into the richest essence. He tells me how, after collecting nectar, the bees return to the hive and pass it on to other worker bees. These worker bees chew the nectar for a while, allowing enzymes to break down the complex sugars in the nectar into simple sugars. This makes the nectar easier to digest as well as resistant to bacteria. The nectar is then deposited throughout the honeycombs of the hive. Here, water evaporates from it, making it a thicker syrup. The bees use their wings to fan the nectar and accelerate the thickening process. Then the honey is sealed with a plug of wax and stored until it is eaten.

By us or them.

But listen to this.

The beekeeper tells me about the dance of the honeybee. When a bee finds a particularly lush feeding ground—a place rich with pollen or nectar—he returns to the hive, and as a way of giving the other bees directions to this Eden . . . he dances. The honeybees dance to communicate where a good food source is. The way they dance communicates direction and distance. The distance is communicated by the shape of the dance. Direction is communicated by the angle a bee will bisect her dance with, with respect to the sun. The dance is like the face of a clock, with the sun representing twelve o'clock. If the bee dances from six to twelve o'clock, this means to fly straight toward the sun; three to eleven o'clock would mean to fly just to the left of the sun; twelve to six o'clock means to fly directly away from the sun.

And the honeybee is a brilliant mathematician. See, these little dances can take a long time. So the angle of the sun will sometimes have changed during the dancing. The bee will calculate the change in angle based on where the sun is at the time of the dance.

Scientists have been amazed at how accurately the bee dance communicates where the food is. Isn't this remarkably beautiful? So I start thinking about this dance. How this dance is the first step in the honey making—in the refining process. And—in our lives—isn't the refining the conforming? Isn't this hard work of life the way he uses to make us more like Jesus? And isn't this God's desire for us, too—that we dance through the refining? That our lives represent the richest essence of humanity? That as we do our work, make our art, we would dance through this refinement?

I think about the dance and how each dance is different for each bee; it depends on where that bee is, what that bee desires to communicate. I wonder if conformity, in this sense, is what we look like when we join every unique part of ourselves with Jesus. This place where we are, what we desire to communicate, our work, our art—all joined as closely as we can with Jesus. We are united with him, but we still retain our own unique qualities, too.

Once I read a pastor describe this type of conformity as the way his wife will conform her body to his on cold winter nights to help stay warm. This is what it means to conform to Christ, he said. *To cleave to him in thought, deed, and desire.*[1]

When I think of conformity in this way, it's easier to imagine that each of us—while our life will be directed by God's will as the life of Jesus was—will express it in different ways. The ways we worship, the ways we pray, the ways we bring glory to God . . . all will reflect the glorious variety and diversity in creation that reflects the very image of God. It is the very best of each one of us joined supernaturally with the perfection of Christ. Because our Lord is infinite, we can all look like him and yet look different from one another.

Conformed.

And yet free to embrace who we are.

In fact, theologian Elizabeth A. Johnson says that the closer we draw to God, the more *fully our own true selves we become.* And she uses Jesus as the perfect illustration of this idea.

In the case of Jesus of Nazareth we are dealing with someone who was more profoundly united to God than any one of us. . . . If his humanity is united with God in this most profound way, what are we to say about him as a human being? That he is genuinely human, and in fact more human, more free, more alive, more his own person than any of us, because his union with God is more profound. Rather than seeing the humanity and divinity as opposites, if one thinks of humanity flourishing the nearer one is to God, then in Jesus' case the logic applies that since he of all our race is the most profoundly united with God, then in fact he is the most fully human and free. Rather than the confession of his divinity diminishing his humanity in our imagination, it should in fact release him to be a fully free human being. Because of the incarnation, he does not become less human but rather the most fully human of us all. (29–30)

I wonder about Jesus the human being. I wonder about those parts of him that made him uniquely him. Did he sometimes laugh too loud? Was his second toe longer than his big toe? When he was happy, did his face blush with joy? Did he have big ears or big feet or long, slender fingers?

Jesus was *fully human.* He had a way of walking that let those who loved him recognize him coming from far off. He had a favorite food, a favorite drink, a favorite . . . story.

He was his own person, his own unique collection of traits and characteristics and likes and dislikes. Just like you and me.

Maybe this is hard for us to imagine because we know our own particular oddities so well. Maybe we have trouble thinking of Jesus the human being because of our deep awareness of our own imperfection. How can God live in skin like this?

Do you ever feel like you are not enough? That you want too much? That there is no one who truly understands who you are? I wonder . . . could this be because we are so busy trying to be who we think we should be that we forget who we are in the eyes of God? Do we look at the others around us and think they have it more together, they do this life better, and they are happier, more creative, more spiritual, closer to God, just . . . more like what we think God wants us to be?

My eldest son is sixteen now. He's always been a little bit different. He's grown into himself in a lot of ways, but there was a time when he struggled to love his differences. I'll never forget a conversation we had when he was only seven or eight.

"If I could change three things about me, they would be my hair, my freckles, and my name," he said to me one day.

We were out running errands, rushing around our little valley, and his words slowed me—jarred me out of the busy. I looked in the rearview mirror at my redheaded, freckle-faced boy named Theodore, and my heart ached.

"I love those things about you. They're part of what makes you who you are. Why would you want to change them?" I said.

"Because they're different. Everybody else just looks normal, and has normal names. Not like me."

I chose my words carefully, trying not to chastise or judge. Something in his tone reminded me of a little girl I used to know. A little girl who hated her freckles, too.

"That's what makes them so special. Believe me, sweetie, it's not a good thing to be like everyone else. That's boring. That's why God made us all different. It keeps the world interesting."

"Oh, Mom, you just don't understand."

Some truths are given little credence when spoken from a mother's lips. No matter what I said, he remained unconvinced.

My son is not the only one who struggles with feeling different. Countless adults battle feelings of inadequacy every day when they look in the mirror or compare their lives to others. Whether it's that extra ten pounds, a secret emotional scar, or a dream that just never has come true, we all have some mark on our being that makes us feel "less than." Different.

I want to suggest that these very differences are dear to God's heart. He says to us, "That's what makes you special. It's not a good thing to be like everyone else. I love these things about you—why would you want to change them?"

Our differences can leave us feeling insecure and alone. Still, there is One who celebrates our uniqueness, One who is charmed by our oddities and loves even our scars. This One sees every part of us and still calls us beautiful. He is *El Roi*, the God who sees.

Yet we, like my son, turn our ears away from our loving Parent. It's too difficult to grasp that he loves us with all of our flaws and imperfections. That, yes, he wants to use the unique parts of our personalities—our stories—to bring glory to his name. We say, "Oh, Father, you just don't understand." But we are wrong. He understands all too well.

Scripture tells us, "He had no beauty or majesty to attract us to him, nothing in his appearance that we should desire him. He was despised and rejected by mankind, a man of suffering, and familiar with pain" (Isa. 53:2b–3a).

Yes, he understands how it feels to be different.

❧　　　❧　　　❧

When did we decide that the morning quiet time was the gold standard? Yes, Jesus rose early in the morning to meet with God, but he prayed at night, too (Luke 6:12). And Paul tells us to pray without ceasing. Do we get so hung up on the way our quiet time should look that we don't meet with God at all?

I wonder what would happen if we stopped trying to look like everyone else—if we embraced our own unique personalities in our spiritual lives. I think the church would experience a revival like never before. Just imagine if the body of Christ were filled with the joy there is in using our individual, God-given gifts. What might that look like to the world?

Imagine a church filled with diversity. What if we did not settle for a cookie-cutter faith-life, each of us using our own unique gifts, our own special way to glorify God? Some people love to pray as they walk their neighborhood, some as they climb mountains, some as they create paintings. Some might quilt— every stitch a prayer. Some might even go after squirrels with Super Soakers.

What if you did what you do for the glory of God? Do you feel the excitement? God invites us to come to him—bringing all the special qualities that make us who we are. This excitement can feel a little bit like fear. Trying something new and stepping out in faith is scary.

Pulitzer Prize-winning author Annie Dillard, in her book *Teaching a Stone to Talk*, has this to say about prayer:

> Does anyone have the foggiest idea what sort of power
> we so blithely invoke? Or, as I suspect, does no one
> believe a word of it? The churches are children playing
> on the floor with their chemistry sets, mixing up a
> batch of TNT to kill a Sunday morning. It is madness
> to wear ladies' straw hats and velvet hats to church;
> we should all be wearing crash helmets. Ushers should
> issue life preservers and signal flares; they should
> lash us to our pews. For the sleeping god may wake
> someday and take offense, or the waking god may draw
> us out to where we can never return. (52–53)

Shouldn't we be a little bit afraid? Shouldn't we let that tingle of fear remind us that we are not alone? That God has promised he will never leave us? This will give us the courage to step out on the edge of our comfort zones. If we believe it really matters—prayer, service, sharing the Word—shouldn't we put the very best we have to offer into it? What are the things you are good at? What do you love to do? Think now . . . how can you use these gifts to help the kingdom of God break into this world *right now?*

Exploring our own gifts may not look like the traditional faith walk. Trying something new can feel awkward. We might be tempted to give up before we give it a chance. When my boys were small, I used to tell them that scared and excited kind of feel the same way. There's the rapid heartbeat, the sweaty palms, the shallow breathing . . . it all hinges on what we call it. The way we name the thing determines our inner talk—what we say to ourselves. Let's call it excitement.

Let me tell you a little secret: God loves it when we try new things. He loves change—uncomfortable, earth-moving, life-stretching change. It's one of the ways he helps us grow into the people he wants us to be. Think about the way he made our world. He gave us different seasons, different ethnicities, different regions on the earth. And he made all things change as they grow. Think about a tiny acorn and how it grows into a big oak tree.

God loves change. He loves new things. Revelation 21:5 tells us that he makes all things new. And you know what? He even uses those times when we are a little bit scared. Because then we depend on him a little more, and it gives him great joy to hold us in his arms.

Invite him in. He wants to be with you. Yes, you. You with the freckles and the spare tire. You with a quick temper who loves to sleep in. You, the one who learns in pictures and struggles to sit down and read. He wants to be with you. God loves you so much he keeps track of every tear that has fallen from your eyes. He knows the number of hairs on your head. (No matter what color they are.)

And he probably counts freckles for fun.

Note
[1] Mark Davidson, "Conformed to the Image of Christ," *Beloved, Shulamite* (blog), July 12, 2011, http://beloved-shulamite.blogspot.com/2011/07/conformed-to-image-of-christ.html.

vii

castles, ziplining, and zorbing

redefining adventure

"Hi all, just back from one of the best weekends of my life. It still kinda feels like a fairytale moment. I spent Thursday eve in a five-star castle in a forest. I had my own butler, shoe polisher, room attendant, steam room, and king-size, four-poster bed. The chef and all other staff called me Mrs. B— every time they saw me, and I was given the most beautiful gift after my talk on Friday: a huge basket filled with the most wholesome local produce in the region. . . . "

I stare at the words scrolling on the screen, trying not to notice the dirty socks someone left in the middle of the living room floor. I thought I would catch up on email before throwing another load of laundry in the wash, but I'm regretting it already. Between the fold of this screen and its keyboard, there is always something that reminds me how ordinary I am. Something that reminds me that this dream I keep holding on to is an impossible dream—insanity, really. There is always someone with more opportunity, more talent, more skill, more resources, more connections . . . more. Women like me from Podunk Hollow in West Virginia just don't stand a chance. Beauty's heartbeat feels far away today. My life feels small and ordinary. And now this—this . . . sinking.

My friend Claire has the most exciting life. A statuesque South African making her home in Ireland, she's also an enthusiastic entrepreneur. Her life is filled with travel and adventure. The week before, she told me and our other colleagues about a trip spent hiking, ziplining, and zorbing (don't worry if you have to look that up—I did, too). And here she is telling us about her stay in a castle. Yes, a castle! A five-star castle at that. (I think any castle would get five stars in my book.)

I sigh, close the laptop, and bend to scoop up the errant socks. This might be as exotic as my day gets: the mystery of the misplaced socks. What kind of maniac would abandon two perfectly good socks? I chuckle to myself at the self-created drama. Still, my mind flashes to Claire, and I feel a downward pull on my heart.

Who lives that life? Not this person.

Claire's heart-beauty keeps me from despairing to the point of envy—I love that precious lady too much to begrudge her adventures. Far from being a braggart, Claire carries contagious joy with her everywhere she goes. Being with Claire is a lesson in opening the eye to beauty everywhere. I have seen her just as exuberant about a tree filled with vultures as she seems to be about the castle. Besides, wasn't Teddy Roosevelt right when he said,

"Comparison is the thief of joy"? But I know myself well enough to see that it's time to sit down and look deep inside. I go to the place I always go with the hard questions—the heart questions: to the dining room floor. With my face pressed against the cold, hard wood, I ask: *What's eating me, Lord?*

I wait in silence. I am David, sitting before the Lord, waiting for an answer. As I wait, I remember that in 2 Samuel 12, David did not receive the answer he desired.

> After Nathan had gone home, the LORD struck the child that Uriah's wife had borne to David, and he became ill. David pleaded with God for the child. He fasted and spent the nights lying in sackcloth on the ground. The elders of his household stood beside him to get him up from the ground, but he refused, and he would not eat any food with them. On the seventh day the child died. (2 Sam. 12:15–18a)

The son born to David by Bathsheba died—even after his fasting and weeping, even after his pleas to God. Not nearly as precious, what I seek is more amorphous.

What is this trying to die inside of me, Lord? Will you not let it live?

My everyday life hums plain and boring. I feel forgotten. I am that invisible little girl again—number three, lost in the shadows cast by others. I'm angry at myself for letting these feelings resurrect. Why can I not rest secure in the love of my Savior? I know he is enough. But it seems like once a year my fragile psyche goes through a bruising that changes me. The year before, it was after a particularly painful rejection from a publisher who was considering one of my novels. In the heat of that discouragement, I had an opportunity to go on a mission trip to Haiti with some folks from the hospital where I work. Only, circumstances didn't work out. The answer was no. Again. I was devastated. And angry. I recorded some thoughts in my journal during that time:

When the answer is "no": Life goes on.

I storm and rage and weep into my pillow. I ask "why," shed tears of loss, flail about in confusion. Grief breathes through my nostrils, slips down my cheeks at unexpected moments, colors the days gray.

*But **love still lives.***

This shattered heart still beats and blood pumps through these veins. I still cook the dinner, keep the appointments, fold the laundry . . . go to work in the morning.

Life goes on.

Night doesn't turn into day, seasons fade from one into another, the earth continues its same well-worn path.

God is still God.

That never changes and what good will it do me to be angry at God?

I am small. Wounded. Alone.

But not. Really.

The question screams at me in the dead of night: What will I do with this sorrow?

What now?

I can pretend a while. Wear this mask of courtesy.

In this brokenness, I feel the Lord soft. I pull away.

"Leave me be," I say. But he never does.

"I'm tired of you," my heart cries. "Have mercy on who you want. Why is it never me?"

And I know it's not true but it feels true enough . . . right now . . . in this moment . . . when the answer is "no."

I am Elijah, under his broom tree. "I have had enough, Lord," I say. When the angels come, they have no wings. Only gentle hands, gentle words, love. These hands that feed and water—nourish my soul—these hands are flesh and blood. But they are holy. God rests in these palms. They hold him out to me. I shy away at first. But I see him there. Waiting. Filled with love.

He cares for me. That's why he says "no" sometimes. Don't I do this with my own children? I am a parent after all. And this sorrow? What of it?

They say the recent earthquake in Chile may have shortened the length of a day by 1.26 microseconds. The rotation of the earth is forever changed. When worlds shake, life is never the same again. Bodies move

differently around the axis. Sorrow shifts the balance.
Grief changes the view.

Can I see beauty in the shift? See with God-eyes?

When the answer is no . . .

Life goes on.
Love still lives.
God is still God.

And sorrow changes my view.

It took an entire year to get my feet back under me again. I almost gave up writing. "Why should I waste my time doing this, Lord?" I asked. "When it seems to take me nowhere?"

I felt ashamed for having myself a good old-fashioned pity party, and said so to a good friend. She told me to be gentle with myself. "I'd say this is more than a pity party and definitely something worth paying attention to," she said. "Something needful is happening here."

And she was right. In the midst of all that storming, God began to speak a new thing.

Do it for joy.

Um. Excuse me?

For joy, Laura. For me.

This turned me all around. Wasn't I? All this—this word-tending—wasn't it for God? It's what I've always said. Have I been lying to myself and others? That "no" shined a harsh light on a truth I may not otherwise have realized. Somehow, this writing thing had become an idol instead of a way to pursue God.

I emerged from that season with a firmer faith. With a sense that, yes, *he is enough.* I always thought I knew this truth, but after that season of "no," I knew it in my heart. But here I am, two years later, with that same heartache. So many people around me are doing big things for God—not just speaking at conferences in castles, but flying across the world to feed orphans, bringing home children from other countries and naming them their own, teaching impoverished peoples how to start businesses and improve their lives and those of their offspring. . . .

"We've been through this, Lord," I tell the dining room floor. "I know this isn't the season for me." But my heart is crying, "Don't you love me as much as the others? Am I not good enough, smart enough, strong enough—enough?—that you would trust *me* with this, too?"

This third child of four born into a working-class family with tired parents—this second daughter, the invisible number three— she is suddenly ten years old again and clothed in insignificance.

Not good enough.

How can such a thing continue to chase me throughout my life? Why must I fight this enemy time and time again? I am the servant entrusted with the one talent in Matthew 25—given only what my little ability can manage. I stand in fear and sorrow, and I understand why such a servant would bury her talent.

If the Master does not believe in you, how can you believe in yourself?

But my Master, he loves me too much to let me wallow this way. He believes in me. Didn't he entrust me with this talent? It is I who do not believe, letting a world preoccupied with accomplishments tell me that this is what God wants.

I turn in my Bible to Hosea 6:6 (NRSV). To these words: "For I desire steadfast love and not sacrifice, the knowledge of God rather than burnt offerings."

Steadfast love. The knowledge of God.

Is it possible? That more than the *doing*, God simply wants me. *Me.*

Do you remember the story of David's anointing in 1 Samuel 16?

God had rejected Saul as king, and he told Samuel, "Fill your horn with oil and be on your way; I am sending you to Jesse of Bethlehem. I have chosen one of his sons to be king."

So Samuel went to Bethlehem, and when he saw Jesse's son Eliab, he thought, "Surely the LORD's anointed stands here before the LORD."

But God said no.

So Jesse called Abinadab. But it wasn't him, either. Then came Shammah. And Samuel said he was not the Lord's chosen. Seven of Jesse's sons passed before Samuel, and none of them was the one. Not until David—the youngest, the least likely of all—was called before him did Samuel take the horn of oil and anoint him.

And do you remember what God told Samuel early on in that process? "The LORD does not look at the things people look at," he said. "People look at the outward appearance, but the LORD looks at the heart."

❧   ❧   ❧

The morning clutches its mantle of dark and the moon still peeks—just a sliver of a smile. The grass is frosted over, and I can see my breath in front of me—long, lacy tendrils that stand out against the dark. I am grateful for this fleece robe—the one my sister-in-law bought me for Christmas when I was eight months pregnant with my first. He's in his late teens now, and the robe wraps around me twice, but it is warm, and it is comfortable, and I am much too frugal to throw away something that has worked perfectly fine for all these years.

I wait for Lucy Mae at the edge of the yard under the smiling moon. She doesn't like the crispy grass, either, and she picks her way slowly before finding the perfect spot. Fog settles into the low places, and a mist begins to rise as the round earth's imagined corners[1] begin to glisten red.

My spiritual director said I was a *name-caller*. And I've been able to think of little else.

"Where does that come from?" she wanted to know.

Her words jarred me—the mirror was broken and, suddenly, I saw truth. I would never dream of calling another person something horrible, but *I call myself bad names.*

The way the sky fills with light in the morning is a mystery to me. I know the scientists can tell me how it happens. How the sun is rising on one side of the horizon, but the other side begins to glow long before she shows her morning face. There must be a way the light is diffused . . . maybe a series of astronomical mirrors reflect and refract the rays until they push out darkness . . . everywhere. Maybe these giant mirrors show truth. I don't know, but the moon's warm smile is growing dim, and Lucy Mae has decided she doesn't mind the grass stiff with cold after all.

I walk the driveway to the paper box and back to the porch; I give her a whistle and a call.

"Come on, girl, it's cold out here!"

The light is spreading.

My director had me read Ephesians 1:3–14. Said to personalize it, insert my name.

> Praise be to the God and Father of [my] Lord Jesus
> Christ, who has blessed [me] in the heavenly realms
> with every spiritual blessing in Christ. For he chose
> [me] in him before the creation of the world to be holy
> and blameless in his sight . . . he lavished on [me] . . .
> [I was] also chosen . . .

The sun lifts up and steeps in the hillsides to gather strength. Before my eyes the night is turning into day. We go back inside to warm.

We've been talking about stewardship at church, and I know I need to take better care of what God loves. The way the light fills the morning is a mystery to me. The day enters slowly, then all at once, the way the light of truth shines into my heart. And I think it is time to shed this robe. It doesn't work perfectly fine anymore.

✼   ✼   ✼

How is your heart?

This I have learned over the creeping years of this shortish/longish life of mine: my heart needs a regular checkup. Because I am of the she-mankind, and my way is to look on the outward appearance. I cannot see the hearts of others with these frail human eyes, but with a bit of effort and some strenuous introspection, I can get a fair picture of my own. For me, regular heart checkups mean meeting on a regular basis with my spiritual director—a wise woman whose judgment and honest desire for my good hold me in a place of accountability and continuous spiritual growth. I also meet with a small group community from my church two times a month to study and share life. I love and trust these brothers and sisters, and I believe they love me enough to not look the other way if they have questions or concerns about my spiritual walk.

Living in authentic community forces me to self-examine. It's impossible to avoid the hard questions when someone I love is doing the asking. It's much easier to live in that comfortable place of self-deception, believe me. I've tried. But the reward of digging deep into my own heart is the spaciousness that opens up in that place. And loving becomes a fluent language. This is how we shine up our hearts for the eyes of God: *love.* Love each other, love oneself, love God.

Not very many people live that jet-setting life filled with excitement. Research shows that the happiest people are those who invest in experiences and relationships—not status, not stuff. I want to invest in the one relationship that has eternal conse-quences. True, unwavering satisfaction in life comes when we invite God into each moment and see with eternal eyes. This is how we find the joy in the ho hum of the everyday—in picking up the dirty socks, in the morning commute, in the carpool.

The wonder in communing with our Creator is more dazzling than any castle, zipline, or zorb. He is so much more than the adrenaline rush.

✧   ✧   ✧

My world is small. This I know and sometimes I bump up against the edges of it. But mostly, I see the beauty God has given me in the small. In small, I am more able to see the bigger things.

I don't fly to exotic places, don't make lists of itineraries, don't keep a scrapbook of travels. . . . I rarely leave my valley home. I do the same things over and over, until I don't have to think to do them. They are automatic, written on my DNA—they are a permanent groove in my cerebrum.

This is one of those days. I get up before the sun. I light the candle and do my quiet time thing. At the right time, I rise and I ready the day for the ones I love. The breakfast, the lunches, the checking of the planners. There is the herding and more checking before departure. I move slow in the school drop-off line. Back home, I pour the coffee. In goes the laundry and out go the dogs.

This day I get ready for Bible study. It's a small affair—me and a few of the bestest girls. I facilitate, so I must be there early. I leaf through the leader's guide and comb my hair, paint my face into something presentable. The books are stacked by the door, and my homework is all done, but I am running late and the dogs ask to go out again.

I stand on the front porch and wait. The chill of the morning nips at me and I fold into myself and close my eyes. The air smells like spring—all damp and moss—and I can hear the earth drinking up winter. I breathe deep and listen. I hear the dogs stepping on the grass, and it is crisp beneath their paws. I open my eyes and I see God.

The world is crystalline, each blade of grass painted with delicate frost. I stand in amazement and wonder how I missed the beauty earlier. I was thinking too small. I was moving on to the next item on the to-do list instead of living in the now. Right now—standing there on the porch in my bare feet cold on the concrete, I remember that there is One who always sees me.

I remember Hagar and how the angel of the Lord found her near a spring in the desert when she fled Sarai. She gave God a new name that day.

I have now seen the One who sees me.

I close my eyes to see better, and he whispers a wonder-moment in my ear.

Do I have time?

I know that I must make the time because who can keep *El Roi* waiting? I laugh out loud at the wonder of it, and I climb the fence with my camera to take a closer look at beauty. The earth is marshy beneath me, and I am surrounded by delicate beads of dew caught in spider webs, secrets given away by the flash of morning sunlight caught in crisscrossing threads. I feel the melting from the inside out as we tilt closer to the sun. I sit in the cool wet and study the delicate pattern of an ice crystal and I am so very small. I am going to be late for Bible study, and will they notice the wet marks on my jeans? I breathe in spring's arrival and my heart leaps. I am small enough to be embraced by this meadow of hoarfrost, small enough to be cupped by Beauty.

And the *One Who Sees* me breathes love into my ear. He does not strain to see me. He comes to me soft as the morning frost, melts into my skin and calls me Beloved.

Small was never so beautiful.

Note

[1] From John Donne's "Holy Sonnet 7," or "At the round earth's imagin'd corners, blow."

viii

love story

yada, yada, yada

His back is a stone wall between us tonight—cold, impenetrable. It's been over a week since we have met under these marriage covers; that heartless thief Busy robbing us of time together. Each day that passes without the touch that is a promise, each night that something takes him away . . . these lost moments are a wedge that shifts him further and further away from me, and it grows easier to close my eyes in the dark alone.

But tonight I stare at the curve of his collarbone, trace his outline in the dim light with my eyes. And I know the only thing that will bridge this distance is the outstretching arm, the grasping for all that is warm and pulsing under the palm of my hand.

In some seasons, intimacy is a fire that must be carefully tended. I stoke the embers.

In the morning, the sky is gray with just a whisper of rain, and the wind brushes through the trees like a kiss, leaving behind the sweet promise of a coming storm. It's a day not unlike this same date twenty years ago. Twenty years ago, we prayed for sunshine all week long. Twenty years ago, our prayers were answered. Twenty years moves slow like the lava seeping through the cracks of the bubbling earth. And then it rushes forth so fast that the beginning and the end are all the same—there is no time to separate. Twenty years rubs up against every piece of me—carving and molding new topography, erasing the sharp lines of bitterness, seeping into secret hollows and unseen crevices . . . making beauty simply by staying, giving shape to deep places never awakened before. Twenty years ago, the sun came out.

It did not rain on my wedding day.

But the wind was reckless, defying the irenic sky, laughing as our guests chased bits of paper and scraps of love about the yard. We were married outside—at my in-laws' old farmhouse—so the trees could bear witness to our naïve devotion. We made our vows with our feet sinking in the earth, the dewy smell of spring still clinging to the air. Somewhere there is a picture of my new husband—after the ceremony—shaking out my long white train like a sheet in the wind. The darn thing wouldn't stay put.

We go to church on our anniversary, and my husband leads me into worship of my Beloved. Once again, I am an expectant bride waiting for my groom as we sing together that beautiful old hymn by Charles H. Gabriel, *I Stand Amazed*. As I sing the lines along with my beloved, the words penetrate deep, filling all the hollowed out places that twenty years can carve.

Oh, how marvelous!
Oh, how wonderful!
And my song shall ever be:
Oh, how marvelous!
Oh, how wonderful
is my Savior's love
for me . . .

I sit in the pew and twenty years is light and new. He is coming. He is coming for me and for you. Oh, how marvelous is his love. How wonderful.

And it occurs to me how much loving this man has taught me about loving God.

After twenty years of living together, I think I know my husband very well. I can tell you about all of his favorite things—food, people, places, hobbies. . . . I can tell you the position he sleeps in and his shirt size. I can even tell you some of the deepest desires of his heart. I have learned these things through experiences, through shared moments and conversations.

But as I watch this man lead the congregation in worship, I see that I can never know him fully. I can never know completely the workings of his heart. And maybe, just maybe, all these years we've stacked up together have made me too lazy to keep trying. Because most days I know all I need to know about him for life to roll smoothly by. Most days, I take for granted that there is more. Most days, I don't think about our relationship much at all.

After twenty years, we have fallen into comfortable rhythms, which is, well . . . comfortable. Why would I want to step out of the shallow water of my comfort zone into the deep pools of the unknown?

Because, Laura—the deep? Only here can you swim. Only here can you feel the brace of my hand beneath you as you glide in buoyed grace.

I don't really like to swim, Lord. It's too much work.

Are you so sure about that, Daughter? Remember . . .

          ✺   ✺   ✺

We were doing our night-sitting.

Jeff was in his chair, and I was on the corner of the couch closest to him. We were watching a documentary on Malcolm X. It was an interesting program, but my attention was elsewhere.

I was having an argument with God.

My husband was an unbeliever at the time. For twelve long years, I'd been praying for him. I had tried everything to get him to go to church with me and the boys: love, anger, shame . . . you name it, I tried it. Only to be met with heated opposition. On the occasions when he had caved and sat beside me in the pew, the man would suffer near panic attacks: shortness of breath, profuse sweating, and fear of imminent doom. He simply could not pretend to believe something that he did not. He usually left halfway through the service.

This night, he sat beside me—oblivious to my inner turmoil— staring at the television as I reminded God of this blotchy history.

"Do you remember what he said, Lord?" I ask silently. "Do you remember that he thought we should divorce?"

"I can't be the man you want me to be," he had said. "Maybe it's best to just end this now before it gets any harder."

Our sons were six and eight. As a child of divorce, I had not even considered this as an option. From that point on, my God-life and my marriage were separate. I opened my hands to my husband's faith. He was all God's. No more manipulating, guilt-inducing silences, or angry judgments.

But I prayed harder. And the boys started praying for their daddy with me.

We had come to this point of don't ask, don't tell. Issues of faith were not discussed. There was this huge part of my life that I could not share with my husband. The most important part.

But on this particular night, while watching a documentary on Malcolm X, God asked me to breach that silent chasm.

Pray with Jeff.

What?

Pray with Jeff.

And the argument ensued.

"You know how he feels about this, Lord. He'll get angry with me. He'll refuse to do it. It will disrupt this semblance of peace we have been pretending to have."

Pray with Jeff.

He was persistent. As he often is.

The thing was, the following day Teddy had a doctor's appointment that both Jeff and I were anxious about. I sensed that God wanted me to pray about this with my husband.

Finally, I gave in. "I hope you know what you are doing, Lord."

Taking a deep breath, I quietly reached for the remote and turned off the television.

My husband looked at me questioningly.

"I'm going to ask you something, and it's very important to me."

He began to look nervous.

"Okay?"

I swallowed. Why was this so hard? "If I asked you to pray with me, would that be very hard for you?"

"Yes. It would." No hesitation.

His jaw hardened, and I felt his anger begin to rise like a fortress between us.

"I'm going to ask you to do it anyway."

"Laura . . . "

He began his protests, but God provided a way. Out of the corner of my eye, I saw Lucy Mae enter our space. She looked dolefully up at me, and the Holy Spirit prompted. Scooping her up in my arms, I moved over to share the oversized chair with my husband. Without words, I offered Lucy's paw to my husband.

He grinned sheepishly, chuckled self-consciously, and took her paw between two fingers.

It was the beginning of a new nightly ritual. Every evening after that, I offered Lucy Mae's paw to my husband, and the three of us prayed together.

Jeff remained skeptical for a long time. But gradually, his heart began to soften. Over the next several months, I watched God work a miracle in our lives as my husband tentatively took baby steps toward Jesus. Our lives have changed drastically in the last few years. Jeff is now the praise band leader at our church. My boys now look up to their father as a spiritual leader.

God could have accomplished this amazing feat any way he desired. He *chose* to give me the precious opportunity to be involved.

But I had to step out of the comfort zone first.

⁊   ⁊   ⁊

The more I step out of my comfort zone, the more sensitive my ear is to the voice of the Holy Spirit. Doesn't love need this? The steady rise and fall of conversation, the making of space in the day to listen to the beloved? The comfort zone is easily cluttered up with my checklist. Even my quiet time becomes about me—*what can I get out of it? What is God's word for me?*

But what if I let our time together be something entirely different? No Scripture memorization, no burning questions, no aching dreams to offer up. What if I let this time together be the space shared between lovers? Let my heart get tangled up in all the beautiful that is our good God?

Can I be comfortable offering myself this way? With letting time dangle loose with no goals, no agenda, nothing to gain or do?

Sometimes it feels like a childish game. The ones I love the most have hinted this to me at times. That I am a foolish dreamer. *Who has time to meet with God this way? Whoever would call their time with God a "playdate"?* It's irresponsible. That's what it is.

But I know his voice. And when I stand before him, we will have such a treasure trove of memories.

Still, Christians can be so hurtful. And I am stinging from the words of one well-meaning friend one day when the Spirit moves the air around me.

Put on some music, Laura.

Excuse me?

The urging is strong, so I obey. I find my favorite album—the one I've been playing over and over in the car lately, the one my two boys groan in complaint against. *Again, Mom? You need some new music.* For me, learning all the subtle ins and outs of the songs is an invitation into joy. It takes me a long time to get tired of an album—the familiar words work like balm over a bruised heart. Even as I search through the names of various artists, our God's tender wooing begins.

Do you know that when we let music stir our emotions, our brain releases that chemical we talked about in Chapter Four—the one that is released when we think about our beloved—the one called dopamine? Dopamine is known as the "feel good" chemical and is important in the reward center of our brains. The intense pleasure we feel when dopamine is released in our brains is typically associated with concrete stimuli: food, drugs, sex, sleep. But the amazing thing? New studies show that dopamine is not only released when we are listening to music we love, but just the anticipation—thinking about listening—releases the chemical also.[1]

I don't think about any of this as I turn up the volume; I only know what I feel. As I cue up a favorite tune, that old sadness loosens its grip on my heart. It feels like God is gently strumming the strings of my soul. I think that this dopamine release is God's way of loving me from the inside out. He knows me. He knows I love to think about weird things like dopamine. He knows that when science and love work together this way, it stirs my heart with wonder at his great design.

He *knows* me.

The Hebrew word for *know* or *knew* often used in the Old Testament is *yadà*. It's the word used in Genesis 4:1: "And Adam knew Eve his wife; and she conceived, and bare Cain" (KJV).

Stay with me here—because this word means more than carnal knowledge. We have to go deeper; we have to step out of our comfort zones when we discover that this word *yadà*, used for the Genesis "know," is also the same word used for the Psalm 139 "know": "O lord, thou hast searched me, and known me. Thou knowest my downsitting and mine uprising, thou understandest my thought afar off. Thou compassest my path and my lying down, and art acquainted with all my ways" (139:1–3 KJV). Verse 23 goes on to say, "Search me, O God, and know my heart: try me, and know my thoughts."

Yadà refers to a deeper kind of knowing that goes beyond factual, beyond the physical. My concordance (Brown, Driver, et al.) says it means "to know by experience, be revealed, to make oneself known, to be instructed, to know or become known."

In his book *Not a Fan: Becoming a Completely Committed Follower of Jesus*, Kyle Idleman says the best definition of *yadà* may be, "To know completely and to be completely known."

> It's this intimate connection on every level. To know
> and to be known completely. It's a beautiful picture
> that helps us get at what it really means to know
> Christ . . . the word in Genesis 4 is *yadà*, the Hebrew
> word for "know." Clearly when the Bible uses this
> word for "know" it means much more than knowledge.
> It describes the most intimate of connections. One

> Hebrew scholar defines the word this way: "A mingling
> of the souls." That's more than knowledge, that's
> intimacy. . . . If you trace the usage of *yadà* through
> the Old Testament, you'll find that over and over again,
> this is the same word that's used to describe God's
> relationship with us. Over and over, *yadà* is the word
> that's used to describe how God wants to be known by
> you. (47)

He *knows* me. And he wants me to know him more. When I
consider this meaning of "know" used in the Bible, it not only
makes me want to know God better, it makes me want to know
all of my loved ones better. I want to take the time to connect
with them on a soul level—to discover their wildest dreams and
deepest desires. I want to take the time to know what it is that
makes their heart quicken, their breath draw in sharp—I want to
share their passions and feel how they burn for them.

When I consider that this is the word the Bible uses for the
sexual intimacy between Adam and Eve, I want this kind of physical relationship with my husband—the one that goes beyond
the skin and burrows deep into the heart. This kind of knowing requires much. It takes a lot of time, a lot of effort, and a
deep desire to love the way God loves us. But, oh, how lovely are
the rewards.

It reminds me of the Song of the Sea—the song Miriam sang
after the Israelites safely crossed the Red Sea:

The LORD is my strength and my defense;
    he has become my salvation.
He is my God, and I will praise him,

my father's God, and I will exalt him.

The LORD is a warrior;

the LORD is his name. (Exod. 15:2–3)

Verse 2 says, *He is my God, and I will praise him*, or traditionally, *I will glorify him*. That's *Zeh eli v'anveihu* in Hebrew. I remember a Sunday school lesson many years ago on this passage of Scripture. Our teacher talked about how, up until this point, maybe the Israelites had been reluctant to say he is *my* God. He is the God of my fathers, yes—the God of Abraham and Isaac—but he has not truly been my God. They did not know him personally in that land where many gods were worshiped. However, after witnessing the power of God through the plagues, through the parting of the Red Sea, through freedom and deliverance . . . they came to know him intimately. He became *their* God. Our teacher noted that the victory song uses God's personal name: YHVH.

Zeh eli v'anveihu.

This is my God.

Isn't a big part of loving *knowing*?

God knows me. And he wants me to know him. I can never know or understand God fully, but I'm prepared to keep trying for the whole of my life.

Father Raphael Simon said, "To fall in love with God is the greatest of romances, to seek him the greatest adventure, to find him the greatest human achievement" (xiii). In love with God is the place that we don't have the words for. This love goes deeper than any physical connection we have with another human being—deeper than any human bond. Paul addresses this in 1 Corinthians 6:16–17 as he tries to convey the intimacy of these two different kinds of union: "Do you not know that he who unites himself with a prostitute is one with her in body? For it is said, 'The two will become one flesh.' But whoever is united with the Lord is one with him in spirit."

And this is what he is reminding me of with the music. Because he knows that I know studies show that this anticipation effect—the one where merely thinking about listening to music releases the "feel good" chemical dopamine—that rush of delight has been shown to generalize to any experience we anticipate that brings pleasure. Scripture says it like this: "Finally, brothers and sisters, whatever is true, whatever is noble, whatever is right, whatever is pure, whatever is lovely, whatever is admirable—if anything is excellent or praiseworthy—think about such things" (Phil. 4:8).

Is there anything or anyone more true? More noble? Lovely? Excellent and praiseworthy? Our God is all these and so much more. When I neglect to spend time with him, when I neglect to think of him . . . I miss out on the *yadà* that he so longs to share.

This dopamine rush will return. Every time I plan a playdate with God.

❧   ❧   ❧

At five o'clock, it begins to rain and he puts dinner on the table. I stare out the window amidst the clanking of forks, adjust my gaze—try to focus on these two growing boys shoveling food. The butter melts in the dish and they grab their things to go. He takes those boys to church, and I gather dishes, wipe down the stove and table. When he returns, he comes to me in the kitchen, scent of the long day and rain clinging to his skin.

He lifts my hair and presses his lips against my neck, presses up against me and love is new and old all at once. I melt into him and he holds me gently, because he knows my heart is breaking, bruised by someone I love, stabbed through an old wound that flows fresh with blood.

His love is shelter and his arms a safe place because he loves me as Jesus loves the church, and a cord of three strands is strong—wound tighter over the years.

Is it crazy to love this way? When I look around I don't see this kind of love very often. And I know there was a time our love did not look like this. There was a time we lived a parallel life and shook off the passion. Some of my friends say that sharp longing of new love is bound to fade over time.

But does it have to? I think about Dr. Bianca Acevedo and Drs. Elaine and Arthur Aron and all their research on love and passion, and I know that all this talk about dopamine and reward centers in the brain and expanding the self—that these are just words and ways we have invented to try to explain a mystery.

Isn't that what love is? A mystery? And especially the love that endures—the excitement of new love and the security of old love all twined together, bound to each other in the shimmering ribbon of beauty. Who can know what makes it last?

We almost didn't make it here. We almost let the storms of life carry us far away from each other. But how do I tell the one hurting in her marriage *now* that these storms—all these things that toss love about and douse its hot flame, wave after wave—how do I explain that these are the things that bind love ever tighter . . . that make the bond even more sacred?

Because we have weathered these storms together—because he didn't give up on me and because I didn't give up on him—even when we wanted to . . . I know . . . I know my pain is safe with him. He is the love of Jesus; in his arms I find holy shelter. Because of this, the sting of pain is blunted. Because of this, these burdens—these stones that are thrown at me—their heaviness is broken in two.

I turn to him, my old-new love. And this is a choice. Because my natural inclination is to just take care of me—turn in on myself and nurse these wounds in solitude. When it might be easier to turn away, I make this choice—over and over again.

And this is a small picture of faith—of my God-love, too—this turning toward and not away. This constant edging closer, seeking *to know* in deeper ways.

Because Love is alive. Love will not tolerate being treated like a stagnant, dead thing.

Note

[1] Sohn, Emily. "Why Music Makes You Happy," *Discovery News*, January 10, 2011, http://news.discovery.com/human/psychology/music-dopamine-happiness-brain-110110.htm.

ix

happy ending

I'll never forget how they came raffishly crashing out of the woods—bits of sticks and leaves poking out of their hair. My sister all wild-eyed and flushed. My little brother trailing dutifully behind.

"We found a man!" Chris said, eyes darting from my face to the hills behind me, as if said man would appear at any moment.

"What?" I asked, not fully understanding. I had only just come outside, curious as to what my siblings were up to. My stomach twisted in disappointment at the thought of missing out on their obvious adventure. These were the things lost to me when I spent my mornings with my nose buried in a book.

My sister and brother proceeded to tell about an old hermit they stumbled upon in the woods. He lived in a giant oak tree just beyond the border of our little forest, they said. Chris had talked to him for a while, and the man told her his name was Hermrette. He said he didn't much care for people; that's why he lived in the woods—trying to get away from the prying eyes of others.

"What did he look like?" I asked her.

He was old, she said. With a long white beard. An image of Rip van Winkle floated around in my mind. "Did you talk to him?" I asked my little brother. Benji suddenly looked shifty. "I just saw a little bit of him," he said, avoiding my eyes. "I was across the creek when Chris found him."

"But you saw him, right?" My sister prodded.

"Yeah, I think so," Benji responded, smiling convincingly at both of his big sisters.

We were in elementary school when this grand adventure unfolded, the precise ages now fuzzy in my mind. But we're all two years apart, so it's likely we were five, seven, and nine. Or maybe six, eight, and ten. Who knows? We were young enough to practice the *expansion of belief* that we talked about before—to open our minds wide enough to allow the possibility of the story to take root in our hearts. The story is the thing that sticks. We had our very own wood hermit, and though none of the rest of us ever saw him, he was as real to us as the trees. Many follow-up expeditions ensued, with my sister trying to retrace her steps back to Hermrette's tree house.

We never found him again, of course, and our young minds surmised he had moved on to another tree—chagrined at being discovered. To this day, my siblings and I smile in warm remembrance of that elusive recluse.

❧   ❧   ❧

When I was young, I found my greatest adventures in books. I couldn't string two words together without tripping over them in conversation, but I grew up hiding behind the words of others. Tucked under the pages of books, I felt safe. Maybe this was one reason why—when I was twelve and my parents divorced—for a little while, I carried my Bible with me everywhere I went. My world was falling apart, but I would cling to this: the One Thing I knew would not change. It was the first time I would read those words cover to cover—not understanding much of them, but clinging, breathing in their life. They were real. Concrete. Stories to live by.

When I was conceptualizing this chapter, I thought we would talk about the many different kinds of play—indoor, outdoor, structured, artistic, physical . . . you know the drill. I wanted to help you, dear reader, rediscover what gave you joy as a child—maybe try to incorporate that type of play back into your life in some way today. I do think this is valuable; knowing where you will feel God's presence most acutely is a sturdy foundation for a playdate. But the more I read in preparation to write, the more this one shining thread seems to weave in and out of all types of play: *play is the acting out of story.*

Children know intuitively that stories help us make sense of the world. Stories have a way of opening us up to the deeper truths hidden in our experiences. Children always weave a narrative around their play—whether inner or outer. It might be the tale of a wood hermit, or the girl who wants to be known as the fastest bicyclist ever, or the boy who finally scores more points than his big brother. Children use stories to name themselves; they use stories to learn about their world—to work through complex questions that are so deeply buried in their unconscious they cannot articulate them.

Isn't this still true in our grown-up lives? Don't we still weave our living around stories? It's the running dialogue in our heads, the words that move us toward the big goal, the idea of the happily ever after . . . we live out the stories we tell ourselves. This is what I tell my patients every day I see them: *it matters what we say to ourselves.* My field of psychology has a technique called cognitive restructuring in which we teach people to identify maladaptive thoughts and restructure them into more beneficial ones. We teach them to rewrite their internal narrative—*their story.*

Why is that internal narrative so important?

In an article called "The Science of Storytelling: Why Telling a Story is the Most Powerful Way to Activate Our Brains," Leo Widrich says, "A story can put our whole brain to work."

> If we listen to a powerpoint *(sic)* presentation with boring bullet points, a certain part in the brain gets activated. Scientists call this Broca's area and Wernicke's area. Overall, it hits our language processing parts in the brain, where we decode words into meaning. And that's it, nothing else happens.

But when a story is added, everything changes. "Not only are the language processing parts in our brain activated, but any other area in our brain that we would use when experiencing the events of the story are too."[1]

Chip and Dan Heath, brothers who are writing partners, call this "a kind of geographic simulation of the stories we hear."

[W]e cannot simply *visualize* the story on a movie
screen in our heads; we must somehow *simulate* it,
complete with some analogue (however loose) to the
spatial relationships described in the story. . . . [S]tudies
suggest there's no such thing as a passive audience.
When we hear a story, our minds move from room to
room. When we hear a story, we simulate it. (209–210)

This simulation in our minds gets us ready for action. When more
of our brain is drawn into the story, it reaches beyond an intellectual level . . . it reaches the heart. If you feel skeptical when
you hear this, go spend some time with children. The unself-
conscious way they immerse themselves in pretend play will open
your eyes. Stories have a way of engaging the whole self.

Jesus knew a little bit about this. He did his share of telling stories, after all. We know these short stories as parables.
When we look at the meaning of that word—parable—we see it
is composed of the root words *para*, alongside, and *bole*, thrown.
Something thrown alongside of, which, Eugene Peterson says,
makes us wonder, "What is *this* doing here?" (*Tell It Slant*, 19).
We recognize it, just not in this particular way. It helps us understand on a deeper level something that we thought we already
knew. A parable gives us the *aha* moment.

Peterson points out that if we look at the parables Jesus shares
throughout his ministry, we see that they are usually without
religious content. They are stories about coins and sheep and
banquets, farmers and barns, bread, hospitality . . . even manure.
The stuff of life. The stuff even children can understand.

I think this is one way Jesus uses to show us that God cares about the details of our lives. That he is there with us in the mundane moments—that he wants us to notice him there. Story—the telling, the acting out, the listening—has a way of intimately personalizing the moments.

Jesus—he knew this. And if Jesus is our plumb line—the standard that we model the slant of our lives after—I wonder if we shouldn't become better storytellers. Consider the familiar story of the Good Samaritan from Luke 10:25–37. (When I was talking with my boys about this particular parable, they told me it would have been more exciting with explosions and a love interest.) This story has it all (except explosions and a love interest): an innocent victim, the bad guys, a hero. . . .

But just think—when the lawyer posed that question, "Who is my neighbor?"—if Jesus had simply said, "A neighbor is someone who shows mercy and compassion to everyone, not just to people who look like him." It wouldn't have been quite the same, would it? Instead, Jesus uses this story of the Good Samaritan to personalize who one's neighbor is. To make it real to his listeners.

The way Jesus handles this situation reminds me of an ancient Jewish teaching story that I read in Annette Simmons's book *The Story Factor*. It goes like this:

> Truth, naked and cold, had been turned away from
> every door in the village. Her nakedness frightened
> the people. When Parable found her she was huddled
> in a corner, shivering and hungry. Taking pity on her,
> Parable gathered her up and took her home. There,
> she dressed Truth in story, warmed her and sent her

out again. Clothed in story, Truth knocked again at
the villagers' doors and was readily welcomed into the
people's houses. They invited her to eat at their table
and warm herself by their fire. (27)

This is what Jesus does. He wraps truth in story.

I wonder how many people who were listening that day said
later, "You know, this Jesus guy, he makes a lot of sense. I want
to hear more of what he has to say."

All because of a story.

Story is a thin place. Writer Mary DeMuth says this about
such a place:

> The Celts define a thin place as a place where
> heaven and the physical world collide, one of those
> serendipitous territories where eternity and the
> mundane meet. Thin describes the membrane between
> the two worlds, like a piece of vellum, where we see a
> holy glimpse of the eternal—not in digital clarity, but
> clear enough to discern what lies beyond. (11)

When we hear a good story—one that reveals Truth with a capital
T, the holy comes close. You've felt that, haven't you? After reading a good book, seeing a movie that makes you cry, or watching
someone you know live a courageous story, it touches a place deep
inside. And God is there.

❧   ❧   ❧

All play is guided by story. Sometimes we don't know the story
until the play itself reveals it. After Hermrette was brought to

life, discovering his new hiding place was the starting point for many a quest. Sometimes, it's the journey that matters most. But, we grown-ups get all caught up in the end goal—that next promotion, the kids' college funds, building the nest egg—and we lose sight of the beauty in the adventures along the way. This is why psychologist Ellen Langer cautions against using an outcome orientation (such as a grading scale) to teach our children. Such a learning method leads to mindlessness and causes us to miss the details of our experiences.

> In contrast, a process orientation . . . asks "How do I do it?" instead of "Can I do it?" and thus directs attention toward defining the steps that are necessary on the way. This orientation can be characterized in terms of the guiding principle that *there are no failures, only ineffective solutions.* (*Mindfulness*, 34)

When eyes are focused on some point far ahead, it's hard to see the beauty right beside you. This is one thing children rarely do—miss details. From the tiniest bug, to the shape of a stick, to the smoothest rocks creek side, children are always surveying their environment for the next great treasure.

It's no accident that the word *question* contains the word *quest*. When was the last time I gave my curiosity free reign? When did I last let myself get lost in wondering, let exploration lead instead of a goal?

In our grown-up lives, we can forget the deep-soul joy of going on a quest. We forget the simple pleasure that is found in stepping out of the usual environment and how this forces us to listen more closely for God. When we let go of our desire for a certain outcome—from striving for a certain goal—our imagination is opened up and the years are peeled away, freeing us to wonder.

But letting go of a goal-oriented mentality is not so easy. Donald Miller, in a book he wrote about his journey to tell a better story with his life, says:

> Here's the truth about telling stories with your life. It's going to sound like a great idea, and you are going to get excited about it, and then when it comes time to do the work, you're not going to want to do it. It's like that with writing books, and it's like that with life. People love to have lived a great story, but few people like the work it takes to make it happen. But joy costs pain. (99–100)

It's not easy, this living a good story. It cost Jesus his life. It takes time; it takes investment. It takes being deliberate about how we spend the moments of our lives. Do you know why Jesus was such a powerful storyteller? Sure, he was the Son of God—author of creation and all that, but he told powerful stories because he was living a powerful life. We need to tell better stories with our lives. Stories of love, stories of grace, stories of humility and generosity. That's what happens when we let go of the world's standards and accept the invitation to approach God with no agenda, no rules—just the desire to enjoy him. Play. Remember those seven characteristics of play that Dr. Stuart Brown identified? The ones we discussed in Chapter Five? Let's review:

1. Play is *apparently purposeless.* Play is something we do because we enjoy doing it. Not because it has any practical value.

2. Play is *voluntary.* There is no coercion or requirement to participate where play is concerned.

3. Play has *inherent attraction.* That means it's fun and exciting. Play is something you want to do.

4. Play gives a sense of *freedom from time.* When immersed in play activities, minutes flow smoothly and we lose track of their passing.

5. In play, there is a *diminished consciousness of self.* We lose all sense of self-consciousness and live fully in the moment.

6. Play has *improvisational potential.* Play allows us to break out of old mindsets and opens us up to new ways of doing things.

7. Play provides *continuation desire.* It is something we want to keep doing. It gives us so much pleasure that we find ways to make sure we can do it again and again. (*Play*, 17–18)

If you are like me, then it's been a long time since you've been able to say you've played by these standards. Even my weekly playdates with God serve that particular purpose of providing the fodder for a blog post. But I am learning to let go of guilt when God calls me to step into a new story with him. When was the last time you let play lead you into a richer story? Why not today?

Spending time with God in this way—enjoying him for the sake of it—makes for a richer story. I want my story to point to

The Story. Do I dare live a life that reveals Jesus Christ as the hero he is? What is the key to living in a way that will aim the eyes of others toward God?

Andrew Stanton, the writer of the three *Toy Story* movies and other animated masterpieces, says it well in his TED talk "The Clues to a Great Story":

> I walked out of there [the movie *Bambi* at age five] wide-eyed with wonder. And that's what I think the magic ingredient is—the secret sauce—can you invoke wonder? Wonder is honest, it's completely innocent, it can't be artificially evoked. For me, there's no greater ability than the gift of another human being giving you that feeling. To hold them still just for a brief moment in their day and have them surrender to wonder. When it's tapped, the affirmation of being alive, it reaches you almost at a cellular level . . . the best stories invoke wonder.

The stories we tell ourselves matter. When we are able to communicate the wonder God drops into our lives, others are drawn into our story. And when our stories hold rich tales of intimate times with God, people will want to step into that bigger story of the gospel. What better story to tell than the one Jesus lived and died for? Are you letting the gospel story lead your internal narrative? Am I? Because when we do, it will change our focus. It will change our lives. When we live our story in tandem with the narrative of the gospel, God is given the place in our lives that he deserves. And spending time with him becomes the most important thing. Letting the gospel story lead our story evokes wonder and helps us tell better stories with our lives. And we realize that it is all one big playdate with God.

᧯   ᧯   ᧯

A few days after New Year's Day, I strip all the beds in the house. The laundry room floor is covered with sheets and pillowcases and mattress pads, and I am thinking about the clean slate. Somehow I can't stand to think of our dreaming being done in last year's dirt—little bits of skin and dog hair and lint littering up the sleeping.

I stand in the doorway with bedclothes billowing, and I see that the dirt of life—the dirt of *my* life—is a very robust thing. We do what we can to write our stories well, to live a good dream, but there is always the stuff of life—the unforeseen interruptions, the distractions, the dirt of everyday necessities.

No matter what I dream, the sheets will still need washing.

Yesterday was J. R. R. Tolkien's birthday, and in honor of one of our favorite storytellers, I wanted to have a party. But our youngest had percussion practice after school, and his brother had to tutor some classmates, and it was cold, and night came early, and my body hurt from the New Year's resolutions. So my firstborn and I took Lucy Mae for a walk in the dark instead, and I dressed her in a leopard print sweater. At least the dog would be dressed for celebration.

The evening walk is a heart exercise, and especially in the cover of night it seems our senses are tuned to the eternal. Each step has a way of loosening the strings that knot us up in what we can see. I feel around inside of my son with questions, and he smiles more readily than usual, and we walk slowly—even in the cold. On this night, I am thinking about how we enjoyed *The Hobbit* recently, and I remember how Tolkien invented the term *eucatastrophe.*

He coined the word by affixing the Greek prefix *eu*, meaning *good*, to *catastrophe*, a word with its own Greek roots mean "over-turning" or "sudden turn."[2] To me, eucatastrophe sounds like the happy ending, but to Tolkien, it meant more. It's the way the hero's fate is tied up in the entire story—it's the redemption in the end that the telling was building up to. It's the happy ending—only deeper. In his essay "On Fairy Stories," he explains it this way:

> The consolation of fairy stories, the joy of the happy
> ending: or more correctly of the good catastrophe,
> the sudden joyous "turn" (for there is no true end to
> any fairy-tale): this joy, which is one of the things
> which fairy-stories can produce supremely well, is not
> essentially "escapist," nor "fugitive." In its fairy-tale
> or otherworld setting, it is a sudden and miraculous
> grace: never to be counted on to recur. It does not
> deny the existence of dyscatastrophe, of sorrow
> and failure: the possibility of these is necessary to
> the joy of deliverance; it denies (in the face of much
> evidence, if you will) universal final defeat and in so
> far is evangelium, giving a fleeting glimpse of Joy, Joy
> beyond the walls of the world, poignant as grief. It is
> the mark of a good fairy-story, of the higher or more
> complete kind, that however wild its events, however
> fantastic or terrible the adventures, it can give to child
> or man that hears it, when the "turn" comes, a catch of

> the breath, a beat and lifting of the heart, near to (or
> indeed accompanied by) tears, as keen as that given by
> any form of literary art, and having a peculiar quality.
> (38–39)

This "sudden joyous 'turn'" is not an easy thing to capture, Tolkien says. "[I]t depends on the whole story which is the setting of the turn, and yet it reflects a glory backwards" (39).

The eucatastrophe "reflects a glory backwards." Doesn't the story always make more sense once we've finished the book? When the movie is over, don't we look back on that puzzling scene with an *aha* and a sense of deep satisfaction? God knows my weakness for turning to the end of the story when things are going poorly in the middle. I just *have to know* how things turn out. And God graciously gives us the end of the story.

Tolkien saw the birth of Christ as the eucatastrophe of the history of humanity and the resurrection as the eucatastrophe of the incarnation. "This story begins and ends in joy," he says. In light of this ending that I know about . . . will I allow those hard places in my life to fall into line as *eucatastrophe*? Even when they don't make sense in the now, can I trust in the end of the story?

When I think about the stories Tolkien wrote, how they embodied this term *eucatastrophe*, I wonder how my life can do the same. How am I living my life that links this story to the great Eucatastrophe? This is how to write a good story with my life: carry the gospel story within me; carry the Love that changed it all. When the story of the gospel permeates my life, my every day, my every moment . . . the times I spend with God drip rich with meaning.

I am likely never to face trolls, or orcs, or goblins. I probably won't be on a quest upon which rests the fate of earth as we know it. But there is always the dirt of life that rears up against me— threatens to waylay this hero from the happy ending.

Am I able to carry this ring?

I smooth down the edges of sheets and fluff pillows into plump resting places. It feels good, this clean slate. But one thing I know—one thing I've learned from Bilbo and Frodo and Gandalf and life—the journey is a continuous series of stops and starts. There are joy days and dream days and good storytelling. But there are also interruptions, frustrations, and the dirt of life. I must choose which parts of the story will define me. What makes a good story?

I will keep pressing forward, writing these pages. Because I already know how the eucatastrophe will unfold. I already know the happy ending. And it is steeped in wonder.

Notes

[1] Leo Widrich, "The Science of Storytelling: Why Telling a Story is the Most Powerful Way to Activate Our Brains," December 5, 2012, *Lifehacker*, http://lifehacker.com/5965703/the-science-of-storytelling-why-telling-a-story-is-the-most-powerful-way-to-activate-our-brains.

[2] *Oxford Dictionaries*, s.v. "Catastrophe," http://www.oxforddictionaries.com/us/definition/english/catastrophe?q=catastrophe (accessed June 3, 2014).

hide and seek

when beauty is hard to see

She sits on the edge of the mat in the physical therapy gym at the hospital where I work and watches our banter. We have been working with her child for weeks now, walking her teenager—her baby—through a rehabilitation program to help heal a traumatic brain injury. She comes to therapy every day with her child—sleeps in the extra hospital bed in their assigned room every night. She has become part of the treatment team—learning all we can teach her, witnessing every change, and clinging to every thin thread of hope we give to her. And sometimes we take for granted what they are going through—what has been taken from them.

Today is such a day. We are teasing each other, talking about our plans for the summer. There is a shadow of a smile on her lips as she watches our playfulness but, suddenly, she speaks. And her words fall like stones into the middle of our light chatter.

"I just want things back the way they were," she says softly. "That's all. Just back to normal. Our everyday-ordinary. That's all I want."

The gym gets very quiet and there is a tiny bit of shine in the corner of her eye, and I sit down on the mat beside her and put my hand over hers. And the moments whir on around us.

⚘   ⚘   ⚘

It is the third Sunday after Pentecost—the tenth Sunday since Easter—and we are still fresh-stepping into what we call, on the church calendar, "ordinary time." The lectionary passage is Luke 7:11–17—Jesus raising the widow of Nain's son from the dead. Here, the good doctor Luke reminds us that we should still be thinking—that we should always be thinking—resurrection. God has always been and always will be the God of resurrection.

The people say, of Jesus, after he raises the widow's son, "God has come to help his people." This is the same language used in the Exodus to describe when God visited Israel, and in the original language, it means something more. It means "God has come near to us; God has come to save us."

This language gives us hope, reminds us that he has defeated death. It fills us with longing for that time when all things will be set right—when death will be no more and mourning and outcry have passed away. But in the meantime, we're still here. Around us there is still death and destruction, poverty and despair. And it makes me wonder if Jesus did not have more than one kind of resurrection in mind. You and I are just ordinary people—in ordinary time—after all.

The power to overcome death does not rest in our hands.

Instead, we are in charge of the ordinary things—we get up, go to work, feed the family, go to the ball game, do the laundry, sweep the porch . . . then we get up the next day and do it all over again. These are ordinary things. Nothing particularly compelling about going through them. They barely warrant a mention, let alone a book chapter. And resurrection certainly doesn't make the list. We concern ourselves with the stuff of life. The ordinary. And if I am not careful, that word *ordinary* can trip me up—give me excuse to assign little value to these passing moments.

But here the church gives me a good model of how to view time. The liturgical year is divided into the seasons of Lent/Easter, Advent/Christmas, and Ordinary Time. In this case, the term "ordinary" does not mean "usual or average." We get the term from the Latin word *ordinalis*, which means to be numbered in series. Therefore, Ordinary Time is called ordinary simply because the weeks are numbered.

But here's the thing: in Ordinary Time, we are not focused on a specific aspect of the gospel story (such as the Nativity or the Passion). Instead, we celebrate the mystery of Christ as a whole—his life, ministry, miracles, and teachings. These days are no less holy, no less important for this lack of focus—rather, they remind us to view all of life as holy. When God took on flesh and became one of us, didn't he elevate the dignity of human nature for us all? Did he not infuse resurrection into the ordinary moments? Elevate the passing of time to something holy? *When we count the moments, the moments count*, don't they? By simply paying attention, our awareness of the holy in each moment is heightened.

Remember the neuroscience professor David Eagleman we met in Chapter Four? His research demonstrates how paying attention to details makes the human brain perceive time as slowing down. If a situation commands our attention—if we find it interesting or arousing in some way—the part of the brain that seats emotion and memory becomes highly sensitive, and time seems to slow. In an excerpt of a book of scientific essays that he contributed to entitled *What's Next? Dispatches on the Future of Science*, Eagleman addresses this complex issue from an interesting perspective:

> Your brain, after all, is encased in darkness and silence in the vault of the skull. Its only contact with the outside world is via the electrical signals exiting and entering along the super-highways of nerve bundles. Because different types of sensory information (hearing, seeing, touch, and so on) are processed at different speeds by different neural architectures, your brain faces an enormous challenge: what is the best story that can be constructed about the outside world?[1]

Our brains are hardwired to scout for the best story. It's part of our biological makeup. When the things we do in the moments become habit, it's less likely our emotions will be stirred, and the less we will remember. Because there is nothing to set the moments apart, time speeds up.

This is consistent with Professor Adam Galinsky's findings, too. When we get away from the familiar, he says, we experience a boost in our creativity. This effect is most notable when we submerge ourselves in the culture of a foreign country.[2] My life doesn't allow for such a drastic change of scenery. There are things that anchor me right where I am: family, work, church commitments. But what if I learn to see differently? What if each day I wake up and see a new country outside my door?

Living life in intimacy with God is a new country. All of my life, I have caught glimpses of this new country—craned my neck as I pass it by. Sometimes I even visit, stay for a little while. But always, always I return to the comforts of the old country. I'm familiar with this place. I know the lay of the land. Henri Nouwen speaks of this reluctance to leave the familiar.

> You know the ways of the old country, its joys and
> pains, its happy and sad moments. You have spent
> most of your days there. Even though you know that
> you have not found there what your heart most desires,
> you remain quite attached to it. It has become part of
> your very bones. (21)

But we must enter the new country, he goes on to say, because that is where our Beloved dwells. We feel afraid to leave the old ways behind because this is what we are used to. "Risk a few more steps into the new country," Nouwen says, "trusting that each time you enter it, you will feel more comfortable and be able to stay longer" (22).

This new way of seeing, it takes practice. It's hard to see God in the familiar . . . in the *ordinary.* But what might happen if I learned to see the ordinary moments in a new way—as a new country, as a way to pay attention to the holy?

There are two kinds of time talked about in the Bible. *Chronos* time, which is calendar time—the gradual ticking away of the minutes—and *kairos* time, which can be thought of as the appointed time—the right time. Kairos time cannot be measured; it is qualitative rather than quantitative; it is the perfect moment—*for such a time as this* time. Kairos time is God's time, the time of the arrival of God's promised fulfillment.

When we speak of the kingdom of God being here—right now—we are talking about kairos time. The arrival of the kingdom of God is a promise fulfilled, and if it's already here—among us—then *kairos* time must be available to us . . . *right now,* right? When Jesus stepped into our world through the door of Mary's womb, he entered our *chronos* time to bring us *kairos* time. "[T]he kingdom of God is within you," Jesus tells us in Luke 17:21. We turn our eye inward, turn out our pockets, search deep within our hearts . . . and still—most days—we come up empty.

❧   ❧   ❧

According to Greek mythology, Kairos was the youngest son of the god Zeus. He is often portrayed as having wings on his feet, showing how quickly he rushes by. Ancient artwork also gives Kairos hair on his face but not on his head. This symbolizes that he must be grasped as he is approaching, because once he has passed, the opportunity is gone.[3]

Haven't I felt the kairos? My eyes are open to the knowledge that each moment passing is unlike any other, and so I grab each one by the beard . . . slow it down and look it in the face. Those are the moments when time stands still, when beauty seems to speak in ways that make my heart weep, when I feel the presence of God like a second skin—the days my sons were born, staring up at the night sky, sitting beside the hospital bed, watching a single leaf fall to the ground. . . . How do we make *chronos* time into *kairos* time? How do I open my eyes to the holy in every moment?

In Matthew 25:40, Jesus said, "Truly I tell you, whatever you did for one of the least of these brothers and sisters of mine, you did for me." Is he really there wherever there is need? Could it be we are able to enter *kairos* time in our treatment of the least of these?

I think about this as I go through my family's cast-off clothes, weeding out donations for the clothes pantry. I try to see Jesus in the hands of the man on the side of the road when I hand him a few dollars. I feel it. I do. In those moments of giving, I feel the kingdom of God.

It feels good.

But I think there is *more*. A deeper level of giving. Giving as a way of loving.

There is this aching need to give in other ways . . . to give to those impoverished in spirit. To give beauty and let it be rest, to give words and let them be peace restored, to give love and let it be a shelter. The kingdom of God is here. Kairos time is at our fingertips. But we rarely notice. All it takes is noticing. . . . All it takes is *being* in each moment.

Why is that so hard?

Madeleine L'Engle, in her book *Walking on Water*, says:

> [B]eing time is never wasted time. When we are *be*ing, not only are we collaborating with chronological time,

but we are touching on *kairos*, and are freed from the
normal restrictions of time. In moments of mystical
illumination we may experience, in a few chronological
seconds, years of transfigured love. (97)

In her book, L'Engle tells the story of a small village that had an
old clockmaker. When he died, there was no one to repair the
people's watches, so they abandoned their timepieces. When the
town was visited by a famous clockmaker much later, the people
clamored for their old watches to be repaired. After examining
the timepieces for many hours, the wizened clockmaker told
the people he could only repair the watches that had been kept
wound. These, he said, were the only pieces able to "remember
how" to keep time.

L'Engle says, "[S]o we must daily keep things wound: that
is, we must pray when prayer seems dry as dust; we must write
when we are physically tired, when our hearts are heavy, when
our bodies are in pain . . . at least we can keep it wound, so that
it will not forget" (96).

Right now, in his upstairs bedroom, I hear my son playing
guitar. It hasn't always been a pleasant sound, but he has been at
it for some time now and has become quite skilled at strumming
his fingers over those strings. Years of lessons and practice have
turned the tinny plucking into lovely music. Why should our
prayer lives be any different?

How easily I can forget if I don't regularly practice pausing to
listen. This is how we keep the watch wound—we make it a habit
to meet with God. Sometimes it's a simple matter of recognizing
that God is already here waiting for me. Planning a playdate with

God is a way of directing my gaze to the Holy One, the one who never leaves me alone—the one who dwells within me and the other God-bearers I walk past every day.

❧   ❧   ❧

When I lift each moment to God, I enter into his time. Each ordinary, everyday moment. But this is not natural for me. It requires effort. And too often I am like those people from Jesus' hometown in Mark 6.

When I consider those people, I see so much of myself in them. I wonder, when Jesus stepped across the Nazareth city line, did those people squint hard into that familiar face? Did they study each crease of the brow, each turn of the mouth, each curve of the cheek? I don't think so. I don't think they felt the need to look closer at this man who grew up among them. They were looking upon the *face of God*.

They thought they knew him.

He is the carpenter. Mary's son. Some scholars think that by calling Jesus "Mary's son"—rather than naming his father—the people were making reference to the circumstances surrounding his birth—intimating he was illegitimate.

So, not only was Jesus a carpenter, placing him in the artisan class—the ones who work with their hands, one of the lowest social classes—but his birth was not an honorable one. When Jesus comes to town speaking with wisdom and authority—well, they immediately become suspicious. A man of such humble circumstances could not possibly have come by this knowledge honestly. This had to be some kind of trick.

"We know you," they say. "Where did you get these things? What's this wisdom that has been given to you, that you even do miracles! Aren't you the carpenter? Aren't you Mary's son?" And they took offense at him.

And the Scripture says that Jesus could not do any miracles there—except heal "a few" sick. I don't know about you, but that sounds pretty miraculous to me. I would expect more than a few, though, given the many recent healings he had done. But . . . in order for him to heal more than "a few," more than "a few" must come to him, and why would the sick come if they did not believe? Why would they come to little Jesus of Nazareth?

They thought they knew him.

His common beginnings do not fit their idea of what a prophet should look like. It was inconceivable to them that God might possibly be in the commonplace . . . the ordinary.

They had heard about the things he had been doing. This story in Mark 6 follows a string of miracles in Mark 5. Exorcisms, healings, a raising from the dead—all done by Jesus in response to faith. The people of his hometown had heard of these great doings. But they let their familiarity with him become a stumbling block—they took offense at him. That is the key word of the text: *offense*. In Greek, it is *skandalon*, from which we get the word scandal. Skandalon also means "stumbling block." It's that thing you trip over (*New Strong's Exhaustive Concordance*, 81).

And they tripped all over this: that someone they thought they knew—someone familiar, someone low on the social ladder, just like themselves—would claim to be anything special. See, if Jesus was the Messiah as he claimed—this man who walked their streets, who played with them as a boy, who attended their synagogue, who helped tend their sheep, whose family they knew and loved—if Jesus was who he claimed to be, then what did that make them? Why were they not chosen? No. Impossible.

Pastor Edward F. Markquart of Grace Lutheran Church in Seattle says:

> The people there that day were offended by the Incarnation, that God actually became a human being. That was the scandal, the stumbling block. . . . We can believe in the face of God behind the universe. We can believe in the force of energy behind the stars. We can have deep spiritual experiences with Jesus during some wonderful night around the campfire. . . . A God of the universe, of spirituality, of morality seems more plausible for the mind. But to believe that God could come to us through some [person] seems to be pushing it. And that is what so deeply offended the people.[4]

That God would come in so ordinary a way—it shakes up all we've ever believed about the holy.

No, it couldn't be true. God would never choose to be someone so . . . common.

It must take a lot to amaze God incarnate—hasn't he seen it all? But it says it plain as day right there in that passage: *he was amazed at their lack of faith.*

Amazed. With these imperfect eyes that I have it's easy to forget that of all creation, human beings alone are said to bear his image. It's easy for me to stand on the rim of the world and hear God in the ocean sighing up against the shore. When I see the sun rise over a mountain peak and the earth is bathed in amber and rose, I shiver in the presence of God. But can I see God in someone I have known all my life? Do I look for his presence in the ones I rub shoulders with every day? Do I see the holy in my husband? In my children? My co-workers? Do I see God in the faces I pass on the street every day?

I don't think about God when I look upon these familiar faces. *I think I know them.* Because of the fall, we are a broken people, and it seems the flaws are what shine brightest in the faces of humankind. Do I dare to look deeper? The image is tarnished, but it is there. I need to see in a new way—to look upon the ordinary with new eyes.

Michael E. Wittmer, in his book *Heaven Is a Place on Earth*, has this to say about our privileged place in all of creation:

> Scripture informs us that the image of God, whatever it is, both remains and is lost at the fall . . . the image of God in fallen humanity resembles something like a cracked mirror. If we look closely, we can still see the reflection of God in ourselves, but it is now distorted by the jagged edges of sin. We still bear the image of God, but it's not as crisp and clean as it once was. (76, 80)

Sometimes I have to look hard to see it. But when I look deep and with faith eyes . . . it's like finding a precious treasure. When I forget to honor my brothers and sisters as the image bearers of God—just as the people from Jesus' hometown did—I might be missing out on seeing him do great things . . . even miracles. I wonder what great work we are missing out on because we refuse to see God in our ordinary—choosing to focus on flaws and imperfections instead. Because—let's be honest—we have no idea who God will choose to work through. He came as a lowly servant. He chose his followers from among fishermen and other common men. His Spirit dwells in me. And you. Why is it so hard for us to see that God delights to make everything common holy?

I don't want to be like the people from Jesus' hometown. God walked among them. He ate with them, laughed with them, sang with them . . . and yet, they missed it. Am I not the same? Have I not let familiarity blind me to the holy in every person I meet?

Is my faith strong enough to believe that God walks among us, too?

            ✎   ✎   ✎

In the morning, I lie on the floor of our meeting place and study the cobwebs on the ceiling. I recount to God all the things I've been blessed to have on my to-do list today. And then I do the thing that my first spiritual director told me she does every morning. *This is what I have planned,* I say. *But if you have other ideas, please feel free.*

Always, the plans get changed.

There are two young hearts who need me, and we are welcoming summer together. The usual schedule is rearranged, and I learn from them what it means to truly open the hand. This beginning of summer brings with it the sweet wet of watermelon on the tongue and more demands at work and home and church. The beauty of this love-busy has me wrapped in a thick cocoon and sometimes . . . it feels like I can't breathe.

This morning the rain falls—a fine mist over my garden—and I smile because . . . this changes the plans.

My youngest son goes out back and stands in the stuff—a living rain meter. When he comes back in, he hugs me all wet, then announces he's going for a run in the rain. It's one of my favorite things, but he doesn't know this, and I feel a tiny love tap on my heart.

Yesterday, I harvested the last of the lettuce and kale, and my husband found a recipe for kale soup I want to try. There will be salad for lunch for days, but the broccoli isn't ready yet. This cocoon feels good but it is permeable, and life keeps interfering with the way I want to grow inside of it. But I know it's about more than the physical, and transformation sometimes feels like the fallout from a mortar blast.

I think about Kathy Stout, who many know as the Caddis Fly Lady. This dear woman collects the larvae of the caddis fly and takes them home to her lab in a little town in West Virginia called Wheeling. The caddis fly is a dragonfly-like insect whose aquatic larvae build cocoons for themselves out of pebbles and leaves in the creek beds and headwaters where they live naturally.

Kathy has built a business making jewelry out of the caddis fly larvae's cocoons. In a controlled environment, she substitutes precious and semiprecious stones for the usual pebbles found in the caddis fly's natural environment. The larvae construct their cocoon, and when their development is done, they leave behind beautiful, bead-like casings. The result is unique and beautiful jewelry that serves as quite the conversation piece. The Caddis Fly Lady takes something common and ordinary and makes art.

God puts all these beautiful pebbles into my ecosystem, too. But some days, it feels like I'm still trying to make my cocoon out of mud. That's what feels natural. But if I want life to become art,

I need to pay better attention to these gems God surrounds me with. I need to pay attention to the moments as they pass.

This, I think, is the other resurrection that Jesus gives to us. Resurrected moments. And when I take the time to look closely, I see that there are resurrection moments all over this place. The dining room table, the kitchen sink, the streets of this city, the halls I walk at the hospital where I work . . . no tall arches or stained glass, no austere organ music or deep mahogany. Just these hands, this body, these people I weave in and out of every day.

I remind myself of this each day—each ordinary day: *the ground I walk on is holy.*

There is holy in the everyday moments . . . there is resurrection in the hallowed corners of my life.

       꿏   꿏   꿏

In church on Sunday, my pastor preaches about Naaman. Naaman was a master of many things—one of which, I suspect, was time. I'm guessing Naaman did not like to waste time. I think that maybe the ordinary moments were a means to an end for him. After hearing about the prophet Elisha's miracles, Naaman rode a long way to ask if the man of God would cure him of his leprosy. When Elisha told Naaman—the great commander of armies—to wash in the river Jordan seven times and he would be cured . . . well, Naaman was angry. He thought it would be a waste of time (2 Kings 5).

When I read Naaman's story, I start thinking about all the things I have seen as a waste of time. How, these past couple of weeks, these time-wasters are the only things that seem to make sense.

It's the long walks under the moon, the whispers under the covers at night, the looking my husband in the eye when we say good-bye in the morning. It's the sitting with, and the slow touch, and the taste of chocolate. And it's how I've been thinking about what makes people happy and knowing it's not sterile counter-tops and two-minute laundry marathons. And I think about the mother praying to have her everyday ordinary back, and I look at my boys with new eyes.

And I think about Naaman dipping seven times in the river Jordan and I know. It's the dipping into these things, seven times, seventy times, a million times . . . this dipping into the things that feel like a waste of time—if we are willing—that usher us into the presence of God.

It's all these things that seem like a waste of time that make us clean.

For who, when these things are taken away, wouldn't trade all that she has to have them back again? To fold the socks, to wash the bowl, to tuck the covers in tight around the sleepy head?

Our everyday ordinary. That's all I want.

There are things that need doing—why not dip in with love? I'm trying to hold on to this. Before it slips through my fingers like so much muddy water from the Jordan River.

Notes

[1] David M. Eagleman, "Brain Time," *Edge.org,* June 23, 2009, accessed April 14, 2014, http://edge.org/conversation/brain-time. The book mentioned is edited by Max Brockman. 155–69.

[2] Audrey Hamilton, "Living Outside the Box," Kellogg School of Management at Northwestern University, April 23, 2009, accessed May 3, 2014, http://www.kellogg.northwestern.edu/news_articles/2009/galinskyresearch.aspx.

[3] *Theoi Greek Mythology,* s.v. "Kairos," accessed October 28, 2013, http://www.theoi.com/Daimon/Kairos.html.

[4] Edward F. Markquart, "Offended by the Nice Little Kid from Nazareth," *Malankara World: Baselios Church Digital Library,* accessed October 28, 2013, www.malankaraworld.com/library/sermons/Sermons_4th-sunday-after-shunoyo-EFM.htm.

rain, rain, go away

when you don't feel like playing

"I don't want to play with you today."

I say the words out loud—hear the meanness of them—and I am eight years old again, bickering with Heather Kimble up the road.

I sigh.

"I just . . . I just don't understand. How can this happen?"

It doesn't do any good to say these things. It doesn't change how it is.

The motor hums beneath me as I drive the two hours to my hometown to say good-bye to a dear friend. A beautiful mother, friend, wife—who suddenly took ill and, to the great sorrow of all who love her, never recovered. We are all in shock. One of the bright lights in this world, snuffed out too soon.

The drive is lonely and haunted, and my minivan becomes a time machine. How many times have I driven this road? I packed the audio recordings of C. S. Lewis's *The Four Loves*, but I play memories instead.

I met Jennifer when I was in third grade. She was in high school, maybe sixteen or seventeen—one of the "big kids" that rode my school bus. All the high school kids sat in the very back— away from the driver's prying eyes. One day, when the bus was too crowded, our bus driver made me and my best friend go to the back and sit with the big kids. I was terrified.

She caught my eye as I tiptoed down that middle aisle— then scooted over and smiled a welcome. I sat down beside her and wiggled in, feet dangling. That was the first time I ever saw Jennifer. She never stopped smiling at me.

That day sparked a special friendship. Jennifer started send- ing me notes, delivered by her cousin Traci, who was in my grade. After she graduated high school, the notes turned into letters. We corresponded all through my grade school days, junior high and high school, and even some while I was in college. We stayed in touch always, even if it was just a Christmas card. Her letters comforted me through my parents' divorce, friend troubles, boy troubles, and just the regular stuff of life. And her words would always shine with love for Jesus.

I love the Lord so much, she would say. *He makes me so happy! I wish you could know him like I do!*

That girl changed my life because she believed in me. She was the only one in my young life up to that point who told me over and over again that I was special.

I always wished I had a little sister. If I did, I would want her to be just like you!

I remember my first dance. Jennifer invited me. She would wear the Miss Spelter crown, and the Spelter Fire Department was having a parade and a dance. Could I come?

I balanced on my first high heels—those fawn-colored sling-backs. A gawky sixth-grader, all legs and skinny arms. I must have looked so silly. But Jennifer just smiled at me and told me I was beautiful. How she did shine in her sash and her crown.

The DJ played disco music and we stood on that old gymnasium floor. *I can't dance,* I said to Jennifer. In truth, I never had.

Yes, you can, she said, smiling—always smiling.

She showed me. One foot out, then bring it back in. Then the other. Now add the arms. Move to the beat of the music.

I drive on and the sky is pale and heavy; it falls onto the trees and masks the nearby hills in mist. Naked branches stand out like whiskers on the earth, and I begin to lose myself in their reaching—all those knotty fingers and branchy arms . . . just reaching. My cheeks are wet, and there are big black crows on the side of the road. They take wing when I pass and I look up into their bellies with liquid eyes, marveling at their wingspan.

What will this world be like without Jennifer?

    ❧   ❧   ❧

I once heard the poet Scott Cairns speak of the need to *rejoin* our minds and our hearts. He said that our fragmented view of self today is part of what keeps us from noticing life's triumph over death in the here and now, from achieving the consolation of true healing. In his beautiful book *The End of Suffering: Finding Purpose in Pain*, Cairns says:

> Such a healing can very often appear to us as a very beautiful hope; but in my experience we remain susceptible to thinking of it as a very beautiful but unrealistic hope, or one that will have to wait until death trumps our sputtering lives. (87)

When I heard him speak, he talked of reclaiming the meanings of the New Testament words translated into our less-than-adequate modern language. The original Greek word used for *mind*, for example, comes from the word *nous*, and it means so much more than our intellectual thought processes.

Cairns says:

> For instance, when Saint Peter employs his accustomed, muscular language to encourage us: "Gird up the loins of your *mind*" (1 Pet. 1:13), *nous* is the word that is shortchanged, having been replaced with *mind*. When we read in Saint Paul's epistle to the Romans, "And do not be conformed to this world, but be transformed by the renewing of your *mind*, that you may prove what is that good and acceptable and perfect will of God" (Rom. 12:2), the word *mind* is again what we are given in the place of the more suggestive *nous*. (90)

The online New Testament Greek Lexicon on BibleStudyTools.com gives this definition of the Greek word *nous*:

> The mind, comprising alike the faculties of
> perceiving and understanding and those of feeling,
> judging, determining; the intellectual faculty, the
> understanding; reason in the narrower sense, as the
> capacity for spiritual truth, the higher powers of
> the soul, the faculty of perceiving divine things, of
> recognising goodness and of hating evil.[1]

The word *nous* carried so much more depth of meaning for the early Christians than our word *mind* does for us.

Likewise, Cairns says, the original Greek word rendered *heart* in the New Testament, *kardiá*, is at risk of oversimplification in our accustomed and limited usage of the word. The early Christians understood *kardiá* to mean "the very center of the complex human person, and as the scene of our potential repair" (91).

Cairns quotes the writings of Saint Theophan the Recluse, "[W]e must pray secretly to God with the mind in the heart."

The mind in the heart.

> This figure, then—of the lucid *nous* descended into
> the ready *kardiá*, of the mind pressed into the heart—
> articulates both the mode and locus of our potential
> re-collection, our much-desired healing; at the very
> least, it identifies the scene where this reconstitution of
> our wholeness might begin—the center of the human
> body, which is nonetheless the temple of the Holy
> Spirit. (93)

I held my hand over my heart when I listened to Cairns speak about these things, imagined pressing my mind into this pulsing place—marrying the two primary ways I sense God's presence. For a brief moment, I felt it hover there—this mind descended into the heart—and my entire self was engaged in a prayer that had no words. But it slipped away.

And again the aching emptiness.

How? How do I hold onto this way of seeing God—of perceiving God and all his goodness; how do I *know* in my spirit that death is defeated, is being defeated—in the midst of all this brokenness and sorrow of a grief-torn world?

To see sorrow with God-eyes is not a passive thing. It is hard work. My mind doesn't want to stay married to my heart—that treacherous usurper of the awareness of spiritual truth. My heart wants to lash out in anger, to kick and scream and weep at the top of my lungs.

Let it.

Excuse me, Lord?

Let loose the bindings of your heart, Laura.

So I do. I rant and rail. I let silent tears wrack my body. I do not turn my back on God, but face him straight on. *Why, why, why?*

And this is key, isn't it? *Do not turn away.*

In Hosea 2:14–15, God's ways are laid bare before my eyes.

Therefore I am now going to allure her;
>   I will lead her into the wilderness
>   and speak tenderly to her.
There I will give her back her vineyards,
>   and will make the Valley of Achor a door of hope.

There she will respond as in the days of her youth,
> as in the day she came up out of Egypt.

This wilderness time . . . this time in the desert where the Israelites wandered for forty years, where they grumbled against God for lack of water and food, where they worshiped a golden calf and complained endlessly . . . this desert time? God compared it to a honeymoon. Because when his people are hurting, he draws near. He speaks tenderly and holds us close like a lover. Hosea says that when God deals lovingly with us in the wilderness, we *will respond as in the days of our youth.* This is how our heart comes to know him as Beloved, as the victor over death and sorrow: instead of turning away, *we turn toward.* Even when we do not feel like it.

Because this God, whose very name is holy, welcomes us to come to him with the familiarity, boldness, and trust of a most intimate companion. This God walks close enough to rub shoulders with us in the desert and, at the same time, remains utterly above us. He desires to celebrate with his people and to weep with them, to give them his rich blessings and cover them with his tender care, because he is sovereign over heaven and earth, over all the powers of this world, and even over the movements of the human heart. There is nothing we do that is too small for him to care about.

He never promised us life would be easy. But he did promise he would never leave us or forsake us. *Turn toward his face.* This is where the light shines brightest. Where the heart and the mind might finally be joined at last and our awareness of God become rich and full. But the process . . . the way this happens . . . it remains a mystery. The presence of Christ in our struggles so often cannot be perceived in the midst of them. Following the death of his beloved wife, C. S. Lewis experienced this feeling of utter aloneness.

> Meanwhile, where is God? This is one of the most disquieting symptoms. When you are happy, so happy that you have no sense of needing Him, so happy that you are tempted to feel His claims upon you as an interruption, if you remember yourself and turn to Him with gratitude and praise, you will be—or so it feels—welcomed with open arms. But go to Him when your need is desperate, when all other help is vain, and what do you find? A door slammed in your face, and a sound of bolting and double bolting on the inside. (*A Grief Observed*, 5–6)

Is this true?

Gerald May writes of this feeling of the absence of God during his cancer journey in his book *The Wisdom of Wilderness: Experiencing the Healing Power of Nature*: "It occurred to me then [when he could not feel the presence of God] that maybe sometimes when we feel most alone and abandoned by the Divine, it is because that One is so very close to us that we can no longer make the distinction" (182).

Could it be that sometimes Jesus holds me so close that my weak human eyes cannot discern where I end and he begins? And how tempting to turn away when this hollowed out, empty ache permeates our being.

In Christian theology, the word *kenosis* is used to describe a self-emptying of one's own will to make room for the will of God in one's life. The Greek verb *kenóō* is used in Philippians 2:7 to describe how Jesus willingly gave up himself when he left heaven to become God incarnate.

> Your attitude should be the same as that of Christ Jesus:
> Who, being in very nature God,
>> did not consider equality with God something to be
>> grasped,
> but made himself *nothing*,
>> taking the very nature of a servant,
>> being made in human likeness.
> And being found in appearance as a man,
>> he humbled himself
>> and became obedient to death—
>> even death on a cross!
> Therefore God exalted him to the highest place
>> and gave him the name that is above every name,
> that at the name of Jesus every knee should bow,
>> in heaven and on earth and under the earth,
> and every tongue confess that Jesus Christ is Lord,
> to the glory of God the Father. (Phil. 2:5–11 NIV 1984,
> emphasis mine)

Jesus willingly emptied himself in this way, opening himself to the will of God. But me? I fight this loss with all my strength, trading spiritual truth for human wisdom. And still, God honors this struggle.

> That night Jacob got up and took his two wives, his
> two maidservants and his eleven sons and crossed the

ford of the Jabbok. After he had sent them across the
stream, he sent over all his possessions. So Jacob was
left alone, and a man wrestled with him till daybreak.
When the man saw that he could not overpower him,
he touched the socket of Jacob's hip so that his hip was
wrenched as he wrestled with the man. Then the man
said, "Let me go, for it is daybreak."

But Jacob replied, "I will not let you go unless you
bless me." (Gen. 32:22–26 NIV 1984)

Am I not like Jacob? Refusing to surrender my will, refusing to let
go of my small ideas of how God should behave? But this is what I
learn from my willful father Jacob: *do not let go.* And the blessing
will come. During a visit to a monastery, Scott Cairns was given
some wise words from one of the fathers in residence there:

"Like Jacob," he said, "you must hold on to Him. And
like Jacob, you will be wounded. Like Jacob, you must
say, 'I will not let You go unless you bless me,' and then
the wound, the tender hip thereafter, the blessing . . .
when you plead to know He is here, and when He
answers you, and helps you to meet Him here, you will
be wounded by that meeting. The wound will help you
know, and that is the blessing." (95)

The wound is the blessing. This very wrestling that we do with
the stuff this fallen world hands us . . . this is the very medium
of blessing. If we don't let go. If we don't turn away.

At the funeral home, I sit with Traci in stunned silence.

I cannot find the words to express the gratitude, the longing, the loss I feel inside, and finally I say, "I've always wondered why. What did she see in me? I was just a skinny, freckle-faced kid. Nothing special."

Traci looks at me with kindness, and for a minute I see her cousin in her eyes. "She saw something," she says. "She saw something."

The truth is, Jennifer saw something special in everyone.

The next day, I am back home, back to work, counseling a patient at the hospital where I hang my shingle.

He had the nurses turn his bed to face the window. "I like to watch the sun come through," he says. And I move over and slat the blinds, look down onto the street—onto one of those beautiful cherry trees that reaches up with red-fruited fingers to scratch on the glass.

"Look at your cherry tree," I say. And he moves the wheelchair over beside me so we both can gape. It's the day after a big storm and the snow is almost melted, but in its place has come the icy rain. Each cherry on that tree is wrapped in ice—each sealed with a clinging crystal dewdrop.

His voice changes when he talks about beauty.

And down the hall, I stop in on another one who is still in his body, supported by pillows and rolled-up towels.

"I've lived so long that other way," he says. "I figure I'll see what God has to teach me living this new way."

And he lifts his eyes to mine—one of the few parts of him that still moves when he wills them—and I see something new there.

"I'm going to learn things you guys will never know in this new body. . . . Just think of that," he says.

So I do and it leaves me breathless, and it's all I can do to stammer out, "Yes. Yes, you will."

As I head back to my office, I think about something I read by the author Elizabeth Johnson. "[T]he closer we become to God, the more fully our own true selves we become," she says (29).

And when she talks about Jesus, she says, "We are dealing with someone who was more profoundly united to God than any one of us . . . he is genuinely human, and in fact, more human, more free, more alive, more his own person than any of us, because his union with God is more profound."

She uses the Greek word *hypostasis*—a word that has no English counterpart. It means "subsistence, or the metaphysical root of a thing, or the firm ground from out of which an existing individual stands forth," she says (20).

And I think about how little I understand about what it means to know God. I think about the things that get in the way of a deep union . . . like arms and legs and fingers and the way they move when I tell them to. And I wonder about such a stripping away . . . such emptying out—this unwilling kenosis and how it can be a gift because of the ways it opens my eyes.

And I think how much there is still to learn.

The next day, the air is ice and I think how cold the earth must be.

"I don't want to play with you today," I tell him. "Today they bury Jennifer."

I know, he whispers. *I know.*

I'm standing in the kitchen, cleaning up breakfast . . . remembering . . . crying. The music is just the background, but then our song comes on.

"I can't dance," I tell him.

Yes, you can.

He's smiling.

"For Jennifer?"

For Jennifer.

One foot out, then bring it back in. Then the other. Now add the arms. Move to the beat of the music. And he takes me in his arms and holds me close. And I don't even notice the limp.

Note

[1] New Testament Greek Lexicon, "nous," BibleStudyTools.com, www.biblestudytools.com/lexicons/greek/kjv/nous.html.

xii

hammock

why you're never too old for naptime

I remember rubbing shoulders with my brothers and sister in the back of the station wagon after evening church. We tumbled into the hatch, reclining on folded-down seats, side by side, breathing the same air between giggles. We would all four choose a star from the night sky to follow home. Invariably, as we pointed and mapped out our beacons to each other, we discovered that we had all chosen the very same star. All four of us. Something about reclining together has a way of focusing all eyes in the same direction, does it not?

Sometimes, after a particularly long service, I would fall asleep in the gently rocking cradle of that car—the hum of the highway beneath us my lullaby. When we arrived at our destination—past bedtime, dreaming of clean sheets to slide between—my mother would lift my sleep-heavy body out of the hatch and tuck me soft into bed without even a word.

I remember long afternoons under the shade of the apple tree—cooling our tongues with the juice of green apples, drifting in and out as the sun played chiaroscuro over our eyelids. And I remember the scent of summer rain through open windows as my little brother and I lay whispering on my bed—waiting for our bodies and minds to drift into our afternoon nap.

Rest.

As I gently touch these memories with the finger of my heart, a gale of longing wells up inside of me, and I wonder, *When did I forget the way the slowing down leads me into the arms of the Father?*

My Jewish friends would not be surprised at this tender ache that pulses inside of me. "You are missing the keeping of Sabbath," one tells me. "Your life is too busy. How can you hear the voice of God amidst all that noise?" He believes this longing for rest is built deep into my spirit; he believes God put it there. Indeed, Judith Shulevitz, in her book *The Sabbath World*, tells us, "[A]t the core of Sabbath lies an unassuageable longing" (xiv).

It is a longing, she goes on to say, for something that is unattainable. For, in this fallen world, we live in exile—separated from a perfect union with God or with one another. Yet, in Sabbath keeping, we experience a foretaste of God's kingdom to come (xv–xvi).

Her words remind me of the *sehnsucht*—that longing for home C. S. Lewis spoke of. Might practicing Sabbath be a way to meet that hunger and set a table to feed it? And so I began to sit with the longing. I start small—Sabbath moments. With each setting sun, I gather a bit of the day together at its edges and be still. Light a candle, play some music, contemplate beauty, and meditate on the pure and lovely things in my life.

These moments take me back under the apple tree—looking up through the branches at the clouds moving slowly across the sky. And I feel the promise of new life; the hunger is sated for just those short moments.

The rabbis speak of the additional soul that is granted on the eve of the Sabbath—the *neshamah yeterah*. In his beautiful book *The Sabbath*, Abraham Joshua Heschel says:

> The Sabbath comes like a caress, wiping away fear, sorrow and somber memories. It is already night when joy begins, when a beautifying surplus of soul visits our mortal bones and lingers on. . . . *Neshamah yeterah* means additional spirit. It is usually translated "additional soul". . . . Some thinkers took the term *neshamah yeterah* as a figurative expression for increased spirituality or ease and comfort. Others believed that an actual spiritual entity, a second soul, becomes embodied in man on the seventh day. (68, 87)

This is a soul *which is all perfection*, he says, and when the Sabbath day is over, this soul ascends once again into the heavens from which it came (88).

I do not know about such things. But when I remember those Sabbath moments from my youth—and when I capture them now in this old skin—I am tempted to receive this rich lore into my heart. For those moments are counted the sweetest in my mind and are perhaps the closest to perfection I will ever come on this side of eternity.

❧   ❧   ❧

When I was a child, Sunday was the day for slowing down. We did not talk about "keeping Sabbath." As far as I know, we did not even deliberately curtail activity on that holy day; it was simply the way the week unfolded. There were no commitments scheduled on Sundays—no ball games, school activities, or work obligations. Due to the blue laws, not many places of business were open on Sunday back then. So Sunday afternoons and evenings were always free. We worshiped with our faith community in the morning, came home for a big lunch, and then the rest of the day was ours to do with what we willed. For this bookworm, that often meant curling up with my latest read, passing time with crisp pages and flowing words. But there was always a sibling nearby, begging my company in some shared adventure.

Community and rest. That's what Sundays were.

And freedom.

The Christian Sabbath is distinguished from that of Judaism by its lack of rules—there is no set way to observe the Sabbath in Christianity. It's not a "must" of our faith; Jesus freed us from the idea that our salvation is tied to our actions. In Romans 14, Paul tells us not to judge each other if "one person considers one day more sacred than another" but "another considers every day alike" (v. 5). And in Colossians 2:16–17, he says, "Therefore do not let anyone judge you by what you eat or drink, or with regard to a religious festival, a New Moon celebration or a Sabbath day.

These are a shadow of the things that were to come; the reality, however, is found in Christ."

And yet, Lauren Winner, the Christian writer who famously recorded her conversion to Christianity from Judaism in her book *Girl Meets God*, tells us in another book, *Mudhouse Sabbath*, that Shabbat is the piece of Judaism she misses the most: "[T]here is something," she says, "in the Jewish Sabbath that is absent from most Christian Sundays: a true cessation from the rhythms of work and world, a time wholly set apart, and, perhaps above all, a sense that the point of Shabbat, the orientation of Shabbat, is toward God" (10).

I grew up worshiping in a faith that considered every day alike. We did not celebrate. There were no birthday cakes, no presents on Christmas morn, no Easter eggs to hunt. This lack of observance clouds memories . . . swindles me out of the anchors for life's milestones. Without the stones to hold them down, my childhood memories drift away. One day was much like the next. There were no special traditions to hold dear.

Yet . . .

As I sit here letting my coffee grow cold, I can't help but remember the sweetness from those early days. I have no milestones to time them by . . . can't remember how old I was or other details. But if each day was much the same, my heart knows that each moment was not.

We watched kittens being born, butterflies emerge from chrysalises, and tadpoles slowly grow legs. We knew the joy of discovering secret beds of wildflowers in the woods, running through meadows alight with fireflies, and seeing our hollow from the top of a tree. There was magic in each moment. Perhaps that was where we celebrated.

When our parents divorced, this was one of the greatest tragedies we faced in the fallout: we left our childhood home and lost our wonderland. We lost our celebrations.

This has equated in my grown-up life to what I like to call Seasonal Celebration Disorder. (I just made that up.) Every holiday evokes in me a deep-seated need to create the perfect memory. I worry my sons will have this emotional amnesia that their mother seems to possess. I don't want them to forget the details of these years. And so every milestone is carefully marked, every celebration built up to impossible proportions . . . and when it's over, the deflation leaves me empty and longing for something more. Now, mind you, I'm not talking about material things. I don't go crazy with the gifts or decorations or anything like that. But my heart is always searching to make that deeper connection . . . to give my family the sort of emotional anchor on each special day that I never experienced as a child.

I'm not alone. And it's not just the holidays that we overdo. Our world hungers for meaning, and we are looking for it in all the wrong places. When I was speaking with a friend the other day, she said to me: "Child A's soccer game is at 9 A.M., Child B has his soccer game immediately following at 10 A.M., we have two birthday parties to go to this afternoon, and then I've started them in swimming lessons that begin tonight. I'm just too tired at the end of the day to do anything. My husband and I promised each other that this would never happen, but . . . it's just life, I guess."

Is it? Is it "just life" to have an entire day booked from the moment one wakes up until the moment one retires for the evening? Such over scheduling doesn't just lead to exhausted, burned-out, overstimulated kids; it leads to the neglect of our marriages and other relationships and, perhaps to a greater degree, neglect of our spiritual life. The frantic pace we set for ourselves and our children in the name of love is actually putting us at risk. We spend our lives striving, building, seeking . . . more, more, more! We equate personal happiness with financial and professional success. With acquiring more stuff. When these things don't fill the empty hole inside our hearts, we look at the circumstances of our lives and settle our blame there. And we long for a different life.

Judith Shulevitz talks about "time deepening."

> Erwin Scheuch, a German sociologist who had conducted a time-diary study in twelve countries, noticed that the more industrialized the country, the more likely a person was to crowd more activities into the same twenty-four hours. Scheuch called this "time-deepening," by analogy to the economic concept of "capital deepening"—getting the same output from a production process at a lower cost.

Scheuch made his observations in the 1970s, but in the 2010s, Shulevitz says the phrase "time deepening" is misleading. "[S]tuffing life with more things and distractions makes time feel shallower, not deeper. 'Time-stretching' may be a better term," she says (22).

We are stretched thin—to the point of translucence. Hold me up to the light, and I will disappear. All you will see are the things I do. I need more Sabbath keeping than moments snatched here and there. Those short patches of peace have begun to feel like stealing time.

So, I let the Sabbath moments graduate into longer breadths of time. Once a week, I schedule a regular playdate with God. It is a deliberate time of slowing down, a time to focus on the One I love. When I schedule the time, the moments are not rushed. Rather, they advance slowly as I tune my senses to every detail. Even the way I breathe changes.

The playdates I keep have become my antidote to the frenzy of time stretching.

This special time I set aside to meet with God is turning my attention from all that striving, all that desire. When I allow myself to see this longing for more as an invitation to commune with God, the fear and anxiety melt away. And the joy in such a freedom is better than any perfectly sculpted birthday cake I could ever create. These Sabbath dates with God become the anchors that steady the passing moments of time. I am able to move freely inside the markers. And the holy spills over into the rest of the week as well. This is what celebrating Sabbath has given me: freedom.

Abraham Joshua Heschel says:

> Inner liberty depends upon being exempt from
> domination of things as well as from domination of
> people. There are many who have acquired a high
> degree of political and social liberty, but only very
> few are not enslaved to things. This is our constant
> problem—how to live with people and remain free,
> how to live with things and remain independent. (89)

What I learn from studying the Jewish observance of Sabbath is this: Sabbath is more than a day off. It is a turning of my entire being toward the One who created me and all things—and away from the things of this world. "[O]n the Sabbath," says Heschel, "we especially care for the seed of eternity planted in the soul" (13).

Eugene Peterson calls the "day off" view of the Sabbath a "bastard sabbath." "Mental and physical health improve markedly with a day off," he says. "We feel better. Efficiency sharpens. Relationships improve. However beneficial, this is not a true sabbath but a secularized sabbath" (*Working the Angles*, 66).

In a video interview with Gabe Lyons for Q Ideas, Peterson says, "Sunday is not a cessation of work. It is a contemplation of work."

He says we struggle to set healthy boundaries in our work because we want to be like God.

> Work is not a bad thing. God appears in the pages of scripture as a worker, and he works for a whole week before he takes a break and rests. . . . Work is a great gift and is part of the whole business of living the Christian life. Jesus was a worker and grew up as a carpenter. So one of the things we can do as Sabbath-keepers is give dignity to work. ("Practicing Sabbath")

When I see the work of my every day as a part of my ministry—as a way to honor God—it is a natural extension of Sabbath. The object of Sabbath keeping is not to increase productivity on the other six days. Lauren Winner says, "In observing the Sabbath, one is both giving a gift to God and imitating Him" (*Mudhouse Sabbath*, 11).

We observe Sabbath for no outward, visible benefits. Indeed, when we cease working it may appear to those looking upon us from the outside that we have sacrificed an opportunity for gain. But as our heart prospers in deep communion with God, the fruit of the Spirit will be evident in our lives. This is the finest of wealth.

I need the calendar days. I am weak this way. I need the rhythm of marking special occasions. Perhaps this is part of my story. Maybe because I did not celebrate holidays growing up I am particularly sensitive to the ways this feeds the soul. Does it make one day holier than another? No. But it prepares my heart to see the holy in the moments that I discipline myself to attend to. It opens my way to *kairos* time—to the ways Jesus changed time when he entered our world.

∾   ∾   ∾

The Bible gives us two versions of Sabbath commands. In Exodus 20:8–11, God says, "*Remember* the Sabbath day" (emphasis mine). In Deuteronomy 5:12, he begins by saying, "*Observe* the Sabbath day" (my emphasis again). Lauren Winner says the rabbis tell a story that explains the difference. It has to do with "the ordering of time," she says. "Sunday, Monday, and Tuesday are caught up in remembering the preceding Shabbat, while Wednesday through Friday are devoted to preparing for the next Shabbat" (*Still*, 9).

I love this interpretation of these variations. This view leaves me in a place where my mind is always turned to the sacred moments I spend with God. It's such a lovely way to focus each day.

Eugene Peterson is less worried about the beginning wording of these commands than about their supporting reasons. He says the reason given in Exodus is that "we are to keep a Sabbath because God kept it (Exod. 20:8–11). God did his work in six days and then rested. If God sets apart one day to rest, we can too."

"The Deuteronomy reason for Sabbath-keeping," Peterson observes, "is that our ancestors in Egypt went four hundred years without a vacation (Deut. 5:15)." If we do not rest on the Sabbath, we will most likely cause others to work also. Therefore, he says, "Sabbath-keeping is elemental kindness. Sabbath-keeping is commanded to preserve the image of God in our neighbors so that we see them as they are, not as we need them or want them" (*Working the Angles*, 71).

"The two biblical reasons for sabbath-keeping develop into parallel sabbath activities of praying and playing," Peterson goes on to say. "The Exodus reason directs us to the contemplation of God, which becomes prayer. The Deuteronomy reason directs us to social leisure, which becomes play. Praying and playing are deeply congruent with each other and have extensive inner connections" (74–75).

Praying and playing. Isn't this what it means to come before God like a little child?

∽   ∽   ∽

In their book *Every Good Endeavor*, Timothy Keller and Katherine Leary Alsdorf examine the biblical meaning of Sabbath. They point out three characteristics of the Sabbath we can draw from Scripture:

> *1. Sabbath is a celebration of our design.* Exodus
> 20 tells us that God rested after He created the heavens

and the earth. Therefore, we who are created in God's image are commanded to rest also.

2. Sabbath is a declaration of our freedom. Deuteronomy 5 links the observance of Sabbath to the liberation of the Israelites from slavery in Egypt. "Anyone who cannot obey God's command to observe the Sabbath is a slave, even a self-imposed one," Alsdorf and Keller say. "Your own heart, or our materialistic culture, or an exploitative organization, or all of the above, will be abusing you if you don't have the ability to be disciplined in your practice of Sabbath. . . . It means you are not a slave. . . . It is important that you learn to speak this truth to yourself with a note of triumph—otherwise you will feel guilty for taking time off, or you will be unable to truly unplug."

3. Sabbath is an act of trust. To truly rest in God is to trust Him as provider and ultimate author of all creation. (234–237)

To be free to live as we were designed to—within the confidence afforded by trust that our Divine Parent will work out all the details for our provision—this is the beauty of Sabbath.

It's about number three that I think children can teach us the most. Consider the tremendous trust it takes for young children to rest the way they do. Trust that their parents will watch over them and keep them safe. Trust that the world will still be there upon awakening. Trust that there is nothing more important at that moment in time than rest. Scripture tells us that God never sleeps (Ps. 121:3), that he continues his good work as we rest. What better parent to watch over us?

But how do we come to this vulnerable place? How do we cultivate trust in our relationship with God?

When I read Luke 11:1–4, I can't help but think Jesus' disciples wondered this very same thing.

> One day Jesus was praying in a certain place. When he finished, one of his disciples said to him, "Lord, teach us to pray, just as John taught his disciples." He said to them, "When you pray, say:
>   'Father,
>   hallowed be your name,
>   your kingdom come.
>   Give us each day our daily bread.
>   Forgive us our sins,
>   for we also forgive everyone who sins against us.
>   And lead us not into temptation.'"

They have been following Jesus for about three years by this point, traveling with him on foot for days on end, shadowing him from sunup to sundown most days, observing his every move—the common and profound. "Teach us to pray," they say. This is the only time in the Gospels that we see the disciples ask to be taught.

And what is it they ask? "Teach us to pray." They don't say, "Teach us to do miracles," or "Teach us to interpret the law in the most accurate way." No. They ask him to teach them to pray.

Somehow they have discerned that this is the one thing. In all this time of following Jesus and learning from him, they have seen what really matters. They have seen that who he is—all of his ministry and the special way he has of drawing others close to God—all of these are fed and sustained by the way he cultivates a relationship with God. His prayer life.

And this particular prayer model, which is a shorter version of the Lord's Prayer recorded in Matthew, gives us a clue as to why. This prayer invites us to address the Holy One of Israel as "Father," addressing God the way a child would speak to a beloved parent. Jesus regularly addressed God as Father in his prayers. And though the idea of God's fatherhood was not new to Judaism, when we consider that Jesus comes to us as "God's only begotten son" (John 3:16), that he gave up his place in heaven where he was "in very nature God" (Phil. 2:6)—it changes the meaning of the address, doesn't it? Knowing what we know about the relationship between the Father and the Son, "Father" becomes a much more intimate address. And we understand that Jesus wants us to see ourselves as sharing in his own intimate relationship with God.

But do you see what immediately follows?

Hallowed be your name. Even as we draw close to God as a child would a parent, Jesus reminds us that we must never forget who this is we are speaking to. Jesus invites us into relationship with God through prayer, reminding us that this God, whose name is too holy to speak, welcomes us to come to him with the intimacy and trust of a young child running to her parent for any need. This God, he seems to be saying in the content of this prayer, is both wholly beyond us and intimately with us at the same time. There is no detail in our lives that God does not care about, and it is his sovereignty that makes this so. Just as he is God over all of heaven and earth, so too is he God of the stirrings of the human heart.

This story of Jesus teaching his disciples to pray personalizes God.

The only way to begin trusting someone is to be in relationship with him, right? Prayer, according to both this passage and Luke's larger portrait of Jesus, is not about getting things from God but rather about the relationship we have with God.

Time with God. Alone. Just the two of you. This is how intimacy develops. This is how we grow the trust necessary to come to God as a little child. Sabbath keeping leads us ever-closer to the heart of God—inch by precious inch, closer and closer with every slow tick of the passing moments.

We are a people who are rushed for time. I read somewhere that the average American Christian prays four minutes a day, and the average American pastor prays seven minutes a day. I don't know if that's true, but if I look at my own life on a busy day, it's probably not far off. Our prayer life is the first thing to go. And then we wonder why we don't hear from God. This is what it takes to make an invisible God real: *time.* Meeting with him on a regular basis. Seeking relationship.

Remember that list my husband made when we were dating? The one of all the things we will do together? The beauty of that list is that it prompts me to look back over the years and celebrate their passing. It helps me remember all the *times* we've had together.

Doesn't God want this, too? Doesn't he want us to look back and remember all the times he has walked with us—carried us—through the seasons of life? God wants to create a scrapbook of memories with each one of us.

I wish there were an easier way, but the only answer is time. To grow in my relationship with God, to step deep into an intimate relationship with Jesus . . . I must set aside regular time to meet with him. Time to play and pray, the two parts of Sabbath. Jesus knew this. His disciples observed the impact it had on his humanity. And when they asked him to teach them to pray, this is what they were seeking.

If you struggle with Sabbath keeping, as I do, there is one good place to start. First make a regular time on your schedule to meet with him. Then boldly ask, "Oh, Father. Creator of the Universe . . . I want to know you more. *Teach me to pray.*"

xiii

the wonderland of God's love

Perhaps you've seen them, too, as they glide across a frame of blue sky; hundreds move as one, inking out the sun as they soar and dive. Their hearts seem to be pulled by some invisible string as they join that great rhythmic dance that spins us all.

The birds are flying south for the winter.

Just last week, a great flock of migrating purple martins roosted in the giant oak at the mouth of our neighborhood. When I saw that black cloud hover and the tree hum with all those songs, I hurried up the street with my dog, Lucy Mae—eager to get a closer look at our imperial friend all decked out in living baubles.

As I stood there in the middle of the street, neck arched upward for dizzying moments, something amazing happened. Those birds took flight. And the way they swooped and dominoed through the sky made my stomach drop. It felt like I was flying with them, and my heart was lifted by their communal dance.

Does it do that to you, too? This looking up? It stirs something deep inside of my soul. And I wonder, is it because they are so close to the heavens that their journey seems lifted by joy? Surely they can feel the very heartbeat of God from where they are.

But it's more than just these winged travelers that gives the lift. There is something about shifting the gaze, something about that tilt of the head, something in this physical posture that changes the ordering of my spirit. I have learned over the years that when I am troubled, if I go outside and simply look up, there is almost always an immediate lightening of the load. It doesn't take the burden away, but when I look up at that great expanse of sky, I am reminded that I do not carry that burden alone.

So here I am, lost in the wonder of the sky, and in my quiet time, I read the account of blind Bartimaeus in Mark 10. And to my surprise, when I read the literal Greek translation of the Scripture, I find this word: *anablepo*.[1] It's the word that in Scripture is translated *to receive sight*. But when I look at the word-for-word literal translation, this is what it says (after Jesus asks Bartimaeus what he can do for him): "The blind man said to Him—the rabboni—that I should be up-looking."

When Jesus asks, "What do you want me to do for you?" Bartimaeus tells him, "Make me up-looking." And after Jesus restores his sight, the same word is used: *anablepo*. "And immediately he *up-looks* [receives sight] and followed Jesus on the way."

Bartimaeus. He wants to see. He has never had reason to look up before, this man who has never seen the sky; he's a man who—some scholars think—is the blind son of a blind man. This is what they think the qualifier "son of Timaeus" tells us. This is one way to reconcile the story with its sister story in Matthew 20. In that variation, we have two blind men instead of only Bartimaeus. Scholars speculate that the second man must have been Timaeus—that father and son were begging together on the outskirts of Jericho (*Commentary on the Whole Bible*). If this is true, I wonder: Did growing up the second generation in blindness make his world even darker? And were there more? Was there some genetic disposition in the family that struck its men with blindness? And if so, how hopeless did it seem, how utterly impossible, to dream of eyes that could see? And so maybe this darkness was more than physical; maybe it was the darkness of a loss of hope, too. Maybe Bartimaeus believed this was his lot in life.

And I wonder, too . . . did he ever have reason to look up? Was there anyone to tell Bartimaeus how heaven falls down to earth at daybreak, how the sun bursts through the rosy horizon and sets the dome of sky on fire? Did anyone explain the way a field of wildflowers bends in the breeze, or speak the poetry of the way the sun makes shine on water? Did he ever hear the mad rush of hundreds of wings pushing air underneath them, and did he lift his face . . . up?

The blind son of a blind father. He had no reason to hope. And yet . . .

This Gospel reading tells us that Bartimaeus—son of Timaeus—was sitting by the roadside begging when he heard that Jesus of Nazareth was passing by. His response tells us that although his eyes were without sight, his heart was able to see quite clearly.

"When he heard that it was Jesus of Nazareth, he began to shout, 'Jesus, Son of David, have mercy on me!' Many rebuked him and told him to be quiet, but he shouted all the more." He shouted until Jesus was before him, and Jesus asks, "What do you want me to do for you?" (Mark 10:46–51).

It's the second time in chapter ten of the book of Mark that Jesus asks this question. If I have learned anything about reading Scripture over the years, it's to pay special attention when something is repeated. There is usually something very important that Jesus wants us to think about when he repeats things. If we look back to verse 36, we find Jesus asking the same question of James and John—the sons of Zebedee. Jesus asks these two, "What do you want me to do for you?"

And their response? "Let us sit one at your right and the other at your left in your glory." They ask for positions of honor. They don't really understand, do they? They are still thinking in *chronos*—bound by the ways the world measures value. They don't . . . *see.*

But this blind man? He does. Because there are more ways of seeing than one, aren't there? There is the seeing our eyes can do, yes. But then there is seeing—understanding—seeing with our hearts, really. The two disciples want positions of honor. The blind man wants to see. And he trusts Jesus to make this happen—to make him *up-looking.* If that is not faith, I don't know what is—this man, who quite possibly was in the middle of generational blindness—he believed. He believed so that he cast aside his cloak—probably his only earthly possession. See, beggars in first century Palestine would spread a cloak out in front of them on the ground to collect donations from passersby. But when he up-looks—when he goes to Jesus—he casts that cloak aside, probably with any coins he had collected that day. He believed that once he met Jesus, he would not need to beg anymore. He cast aside that which hindered him from going to Jesus, and he looked up.

It makes me wonder if the more we have to set our eyes on, the blinder our hearts become. It makes me wonder what gets in the way of turning to Jesus for those of us who can see with our eyes.

You see, there are things that get in the way of this kind of seeing. I think maybe this is the lesson Jesus is teaching us when he repeats that question, "What do you want me to do for you?" We must be careful about where we set our eyes, mustn't we? Because there are too many things that can make us blind. It can be little things—those daily hassles that distract the eye, the busyness that keeps us from slowing to allow the eyes of our hearts to open. Or it can be something big—anger, bitterness, unforgiveness, loss—anything that turns our hearts to stone. Anything that keeps us from *up-looking*—from turning to Jesus. These are the things that can blind the eyes of our hearts.

And, just as Bartimaeus cast off his cloak as he eagerly and with great faith approached Jesus, we must cast off all these things that hinder us from coming to Jesus—from having our sight restored to eternal vision. What is keeping us from drawing near to Jesus? Is it money? Possessions? Fear? A diagnosis, maybe? Look up. Let's be up-looking . . . let's look to Jesus and let nothing hinder us.

In previous chapters, we've talked about legalism, the God-shaped hole, the impact of stepping into the new, keeping our eyes open to beauty, and the importance of keeping Sabbath.

We've considered what it means to come to God like a little child and how to tell a good story with our lives. I've shared parts of my story and how these things have helped me draw closer to God and grow in intimacy with him. But what about you, dear reader? Maybe you don't need such drastic measures. Perhaps— for you—falling in love with the Holy One is as simple as falling out of bed each morning.

I do not doubt that we come to God in different ways. When Jesus died on the cross, the veil of the temple was torn. Not only does this signify that Christ's death is ample atonement for sin, but it also shows that the veil of sin no longer keeps us from approaching the Holy of Holies—the place where God dwells— directly. We are not bound by any ritual or human action to make us worthy enough to do so. Christ's sacrifice is enough. When I encourage you to plan a playdate with God, I am by no means saying this is the only way to grow in intimacy with God. But my question for you is this: What is the way for you?

If you are like me, you need these tangible reminders. I am bound by the weaknesses of this frail humanity. I am easily dis- tracted, my attention falters, I quickly forget the many significant gestures of love the Father has demonstrated to me over the long years of my life. I take those I love the most for granted and, often, they are the ones who will feel the brunt of my anger or carelessness. This is what it means to be human. In my quest for the blue flower, my eyes overlook the many gifts of beauty I pass in my journeying. I forget the wonder there is in each blade of grass, in each up-turned leaf, in each curve of the face. There is wonder in each passing moment because God's fingerprints are all over them.

Henry van Dyke, in the introduction to his collection of short stories that he called *The Blue Flower,* says this about writing:

> [W]hen one wishes to write about life, especially about that part of it which is inward, the inwrought experience of living may be of value. And that is a thing which one cannot get in haste, neither can it be made to order. Patient waiting belongs to it; and rainy days belong to it; and the best of it sometimes comes in the doing of tasks that seem not to amount to much. So in the long run, I suppose, while delay and failure and interruption may keep a piece of work very small, yet in the end they enter into the quality of it and bring it a little nearer to the real thing, which is always more or less of a secret. (2)

The best of it sometimes comes in the doing of tasks that seem not to amount to much.

The same is true for our spiritual lives, I think. It's these things we do that don't seem to amount to much on the surface—the everyday stuff, the ways we pass the moments in the ordinary—these are doing the inner work of binding our hearts to God's and changing the way we look at the world. Changing the way we look at each other.

Because it's about where I fix my eyes—it's about *seeing.* And too many days I don't see beyond the dusty corners of my world—mounds of laundry, hungry mouths, broken hearts and bodies. I am nearsighted—blinded by everything I can put arms around. These are the things that grow dim, that I trip over every day as

I stumble through life. Go to work, pay the bills, clean the house, mow the lawn. . . .

There are real things that can't be touched or seen.

There are things so high they cannot be cupped in a hand. Things so wonder-full they are easy to miss. Because they require more than a distracted glance.

To keep my eyes open wide to wonder . . . *I must shift the eyes of my heart.* I must become up-looking. I must look to Jesus.

❧   ❧   ❧

What do I want Jesus to do for me?

I want to be up-looking. That's what *Playdates with God* is all about.

I want to see. All this chasing the Blue Flower, this running after God.

I want to see.

Note

[1] I like to use an online interlinear Bible from the website *Scripture4All. org*. The URL for Mark 10 is www.scripture4all.org/OnlineInterlinear/NTpdf/mar10.pdf.

postscript

The beach is wide here—the ocean's arm long and clumsy. She drops many treasures as she draws away from shore. The waters are reluctant and clinging, and I splash through lingering tidal pools—peer through their glass surfaces at the gifts their mother sea leaves behind. We are on our family vacation by the sea, and I am doing those two things I love to do when we perch for a time on the rim of our world: watch for the birthing of light and talk with God.

But in the waiting, I am distracted by the discards of the sea, and before long my hands are full of cockleshells and memories of things once living. I am looking for a special shell—a promise to carry with me. The pieces of the sea snail spirals draw me (shark's eye is what they are called, the tourist guide tells me)—such a twisted up, spiraling, crazy kind of beauty. I cannot find a whole one, and as I trace my thumb along the broken circle, I outline the course of my life.

I think about the oyster shell and the story of how the pearl is made by the irritant that sneaks into hidden places. I turn over a stray with my toes. The underneath is a blush—this beautiful rose buried in the sand. If I hadn't looked closer, all I would have seen is the beige fanning out. I stick Rose in my pocket.

Luci Shaw says that, to her, "[S]hells are a parable of personal choice and significance." She says, "[T]he incident of noticing it in its own setting and taking it for my own renders it notable; its selection is part of its history" (100).

So I am writing history.

I wade through the warm tidal pools, peering through the water-pane at another world. Tiny fish scatter in my wake, darting to and fro so quickly I cannot tell what they look like. I don't know what they are named, but they remind me of pale visions of the minnows in my creek back home. I follow them—step gingerly. They have tiny, black stripes down the side of a translucent body. The little pool is not very big, and they swim to the lip of it and then away again. I wonder if they are confused by this sudden shrinking of the ocean. They ghost away and I move on.

I could wander this way for hours—exploring this wide stretch of sand. It is ever-changing. I come upon another bed of shells and move my eyes over them, searching for that circular eye. The diversity of colors and shapes and patterns takes my breath, and I tell God how lovely it is that he put so much care in the making of his world. I think of the little-girl me, and I cry, knowing the care he puts into us. I thank him in a whisper, sing him a song—let my voice drift over the crashing waves and lift to heaven.

The gray parts of the day shimmer silver here and wink with secrets from the deep. It's a strange sort of contrast how the vastness of this beauty can remind me how small I am and how treasured I am at the same time. So many times I have come to the sea and been filled with words that spill out on the page the way the ocean laps over the shore. But this time . . . I have been listening. There was a time when meeting God here ushered me into a sacred place. My mind would slow and my body relax. All the world became beauty as I centered on him. But this time, I feel no such shift. It frightens me at first. *Are you hiding from me?* I ask him. But his presence is strong within me, pulsing with each beat of my heart. And I realize that he has become so dear to me that the place we meet no longer matters. I carry him inside of me and so every place is sacred.

I have been meeting with God for a weekly playdate for almost three years now. Those times I set apart to focus on our love have become almost indistinguishable from the everyday in my mind. For it is impossible to cultivate such intimacy and then turn it off again. My life has become a playdate. He is my most constant companion. Oh yes, there are times when my gaze still shifts to worldly things. This will probably be so until I pass into glory. I am finite. Fallible. But practicing falling in love with God has changed me. It is still changing me.

Eugene Peterson says it this way: "There is a large, leisurely center to existence where God must be deeply pondered, lovingly believed. This demand is not for prayer-on-the-run or for prayer-on-request. It means entering realms of spirit where wonder and adoration have space to develop, where play and delight have time to flourish" (*Working the Angles*, 65).

This morning—as I wait for that red orbed sun to catch the sky on fire—I write the names of some of the people I love in the sand. It's the way I like to pray here. As the sun rises higher in the sky, dropping diamonds on the water in its wake, I take my shell-pencil and write my dreams there, too. And when the ocean comes up with her wet fingers and wipes away those letters . . . I feel the weight of them carried safe in her belly—off to faraway places I can only guess—safely held by the Dreamgiver.

Yesterday, as we sat looking out over the ocean in the early morning, I said to my boys, "Look at the way the water glistens when the sun falls just so—like a cloak made of millions of diamonds." I told them I want to take a basket and pluck each diamond one by one—gather light and beauty. And then I said, *We will be rich beyond measure.*

But even as I said it I knew. Oh, how rich we are. Rich with light and love. These sun-filled days don't make me more so.

They only allow the moments, like diamonds, to shine in my heart.

references

Acevedo, Bianca P., Arthur Aron, Helen E. Fisher, and Lucy L. Brown. "Neural Correlates of Long-Term Intense Romantic Love." *Social Cognitive and Affective Neuroscience* 7, no. 2 (2012):145–159. doi:10.1093/scan/nsq092.

Aron, Elaine N., and Arthur Aron. "Love and Expansion of the Self: The State of the Model." *Personal Relationships* 3, no. 1 (1996): 45–58.

Augustine. *The Confessions of St. Augustine.* Translated by Henry Chadwick. Oxford: Oxford University Press, 1991. Kindle edition.

Barclay, William. *The New Daily Study Bible: The Gospel of Matthew,* vol. 1. Edinburgh: Saint Andrew Press, 2001. Kindle edition.

Benaroch, Roy, ed. "Piaget Stages of Development." *WebMD.* November 6, 2012. http://children.webmd.com/piaget-stages-of-development.

Brannen, Barbara. *The Gift of Play: Why Adult Women Stop Playing and How to Start Again.* Lincoln, NE: Writers Club Press, 2002.

Brooks, David. *The Social Animal: The Hidden Sources of Love, Character, and Achievement.* New York: Random House, 2011.

Brown, Driver, Briggs and Gesenius. "Hebrew Lexicon entry for Yadà." "The NAS Old Testament Hebrew Lexicon." http://www.biblestudytools.com/lexicons/hebrew/nas/yada.html. Accessed 2014.

Brown, Stuart. *Play: How It Shapes the Brain, Opens the Imagination, and Invigorates the Soul.* New York: Avery, 2009.

Cairns, Scott. *The End of Suffering: Finding Purpose in Pain.* Brewster, MA: Paraclete Press, 2009.

Coleridge, Samuel Taylor. *Biographia Literaria.* Reprint of the 1817 version, Project Gutenberg, 2004. www.gutenberg.org/files/6081/6081-h/6081-h.htm.

DeMuth, Mary E. *Thin Places: A Memoir.* Grand Rapids, MI: Zondervan, 2010.

Dillard, Annie. *An American Childhood.* New York: HarperCollins. Reprinted as Harper Perennial edition, 2008.

————. *Teaching a Stone to Talk.* New York: HarperCollins. Reprinted as Harper Perennial edition, 2008.

Dutton, D. G., and A. P. Aron. "Some Evidence for Heightened Sexual Attraction under Conditions of High Anxiety." *Journal of Personality and Social Psychology* 30 (1974): 510–517.

Foster, Richard J. *Prayer: Finding the Heart's True Home.* New York: HarperSanFrancisco, 1992.

Gottman, John M., and Nan Silver. *The Seven Principles for Making Marriage Work: A Practical Guide from the Country's Foremost Relationship Expert.* New York: Three Rivers Press. Kindle edition, 2011.

Hamilton, Audrey. "Living Outside the Box." *Kellog School of Management.* April 23, 2009. http://www.kellogg.northwestern.edu/news_articles/2009/galinskyresearch.aspx.

Heath, Chip, and Dan Heath. *Made to Stick: Why Some Ideas Survive and Others Die.* New York: Random House, 2008.

Henry, Matthew. *Commentary on the Whole Bible*, vol. 5. Reprint of the 1721 version. Reprinted at Christian Classics Ethereal Library. www.ccel.org/ccel/henry/mhc5.Mark.xi.html. Accessed 2013.

Heschel, Abraham Joshua. *The Sabbath.* New York: Farrar, Straus and Giroux, 1979.

Idleman, Kyle. *Not a Fan: Becoming a Completely Committed Follower of Jesus.* Grand Rapids, MI: Zondervan, 2011. Kindle edition.

Johnson, Elizabeth A. *Consider Jesus: Waves of Renewal in Christology.* New York: Crossroad Publishing, 1990.

Keller, Timothy. *Every Good Endeavor: Connecting Your Work to God's Work.* With Katherine Leary Alsdorf. New York: Dutton, 2012.

Langer, Ellen J. *Mindfulness.* Cambridge: Da Capo Press, 1989.

L'Engle, Madeleine. *Walking on Water: Reflections on Faith and Art.* New York: North Point Press, 1980.

Lewis, C. S. *A Grief Observed.* New York: HarperCollins, 1961.

————. *Letters of C. S. Lewis.* Edited by W. H. Lewis. New York: Harcourt Brace & World, 1966.

May, Gerald G. *The Wisdom of Wilderness: Experiencing the Healing Power of Nature.* San Francisco: HarperCollins, 2006.

Miller, Donald. *A Million Miles in a Thousand Years: What I Learned while Editing my Life.* Nashville: Thomas Nelson, 2009.

Nouwen, Henri. *The Inner Voice of Love: A Journey through Anguish to Freedom.* New York: Doubleday, 1996.

Novalis. *Heinrich von Ofterdingen: A Novel.* Translated by Palmer Hilty. Reprint, Prospect Heights, IL: Waveland Press, 1990.

Pascal, Blaise. *Pensées: Thoughts on God, Religion, and Wagers.* Translated by W. F. Trotter. Tarlton, OH: Suzeteo Enterprises, 2010. Kindle edition.

Peterson, Eugene. *Working the Angles: The Shape of Pastoral Integrity.* Grand Rapids, MI: William B. Eerdmans, 1987.

————. *Tell It Slant: A Conversation on the Language of Jesus in His Stories and Prayers.* Grand Rapids, MI: William B. Eerdmans, 2008.

————. "Practicing Sabbath." February 28, 2012. Interview by Gabe Lyons; 1:01. Q Ideas video. Accessed October 27, 2013. www.qideas.org/practices/live/showing.aspx.

Shaw, Luci. *Breath for the Bones: Art, Imagination, and Spirit.* Nashville: Thomas Nelson, 2007.

Shulevitz, Judith. *The Sabbath World: Glimpses of a Different Order of Time.* New York: Random House, 2010.

Simmons, Annette. *The Story Factor: Inspiration, Influence, and Persuasion through the Art of Storytelling.* New York: Basic Books, 2001.

Simon, Raphael. *The Glory of Thy People: The Story of a Conversion.* New Hope, KY: Remnant of Israel, 1986.

Stanton, Andrew. "The Clues to a Great Story." *TED.com* video. www.ted.com/talks/andrew_stanton_the_clues_to_a_great_story#. March 2012.

Stendhal. *Love.* Translated by Gilbert and Suzanne Sale. London: Merlin Press. Reprinted, London: Penguin Books, 1975. Kindle edition reprinted with Further Reading, 2004.

Strong, James. *The New Strong's Exhaustive Concordance of the Bible.* Nashville: Thomas Nelson, 1996.

Tolkien, J. R. R. "On Fairy Stories." *Essays Presented to Charles Williams.* Oxford: Oxford University Press, 1947.

Van Dyke, Henry. *The Blue Flower.* Reprint of the 1902 New York edition, Project Gutenberg, 2008. www.gutenberg.org/catalog/world/readfile?fk_files=3143164.

Winner, Lauren F. *Mudhouse Sabbath: An Invitation to a Life of Spiritual Discipline.* Brewster, MA: Paraclete Press, 2003.

—————. *Still: Notes on a Mid-Faith Crisis.* New York: HarperOne, 2012.

Wittmer, Michael E. *Heaven Is a Place on Earth: Why Everything You Do Matters to God.* Grand Rapids, MI: Zondervan, 2004.